EDWARD D. ANDREWS

GODLY WISDOM SPEAKS

FORTY DEVOTIONALS FROM THE
BOOK OF PROVERBS FOR
MANEUVERING THROUGH LIFE

GODLY WISDOM SPEAKS

FORTY DEVOTIONALS FROM THE BOOK OF PROVERB FOR MANEUVERING THROUGH LIFE

Edward D. Andrews

Christian Publishing House
Cambridge, Ohio

CHRISTIAN PUBLISHING HOUSE
CONSERVATIVE CHRISTIAN BOOKS
APOLOGETIC DEFENSE OF GOD, THE
FAITH, THE BIBLE, AND CHRISTIANITY

Copyright © 2019 Edward D. Andrews

All rights reserved. Except for brief quotations in articles, other publications, book reviews, and blogs, no part of this book may be reproduced in any manner without prior written permission from the publishers. For information, write,

support@christianpublishers.org

Unless otherwise stated, scripture quotations are from The Holy Bible, Updated American Standard Version®, copyright © 2018 by Christian Publishing House, Professional Christian Publishing of the Good News. All rights reserved.

GODLY WISDOM SPEAKS: *FORTY DEVOTIONALS FROM THE BOOK OF PROVERB FOR MANEUVERING THROUGH LIFE* by Edward D. Andrews

ISBN-13: 978-1-949586-82-4

ISBN-10: 1-949586-82-0

Table of Contents

INTRODUCTION The Meaning of Proverbs .8
Authorship 8
Historical Setting (Bible Background) 9
Literary Form 10
Authenticity 11
Purpose 11
Place and Date of Writing 12
Interpreting Proverbs 12
REVIEW QUESTIONS Introduction 27

PROVERBS 10:11 Life Giving Wisdom or Life Destroying Ignorance 29

PROVERBS 3:5-6 Make Personal Decisions Wisely 31

PROVERBS 1:7 The Beginning of Knowledge 34

PROVERBS 4:18-19 Mental Darkness 37

PROVERBS 10:22 Enough Is Enough 40

PROVERBS 12:18 Do Your Words Stab or Heal? ... 42

PROVERBS 13:20 The Powerful Effect of Friends .. 44

PROVERBS 9:4-6 Leaving Your Old Ways for the Ways of Wisdom 47

PROVERBS 9:7-9 Be Wise and Accept Constructive Counsel 51

PROVERBS 4:23 Safeguard Your Heart 55

PROVERBS 27:11 We Can Find Real Purpose In Life 57

PROVERBS 8:13 Turn Away from Morally Objectionable Behavior 64

PROVERBS 19:20 Become Wiser Throughout Your Life Until You Are Wise..66

PROVERBS 3:13 Happy Is the One Who Finds Wisdom 68

PROVERBS 8:10-11 Wisdom Is More Precious Than All Else 70

PROVERBS 9:10 We Cannot Have Wisdom Without Knowledge..72

PROVERBS 6:25-26 Do Not Desire the Immoral Woman's Beauty..74

PROVERBS 12:1 Discipline is Absolutely Necessary 79

PROVERBS 24:3-4 Knowledge, Wisdom and Understanding Brings Precious and Pleasant Qualities...82

PROVERBS 10:8-9 The Wise of Heart or the One Foolish of Lips..85

PROVERBS 12:24 The One Working Hard Succeeds 89

PROVERBS 11:30 The Righteous One Is Capturing Souls and Is Rewarded 91

PROVERBS 9:11-12 You Will Reap What You Sow 94

PROVERBS 10:8-9 The Wise of Heart or the One Foolish of Lips..96

PROVERBS 2:6-8 God Gives Wisdom to His Holy Ones 100

PROVERBS 2:9 Understanding What is Ethically and Morally Right and What is Wrong 102

PROVERBS 9:1-2 The Way of Wisdom................. 104

PROVERBS 6:20-22 Principles, Teachings, and Rules are to Guide and Protect.. 107

PROVERBS 10:29 How God Deals with You Today 110

PROVERBS 5:12-13 I Have Paid a High Price 111

PROVERBS 11:15 Use Material Assets Wisely.........113

PROVERBS 6:1-3 Deliver Yourself from Foolish Pledges..116

PROVERBS 12:16 The Wise Person Pauses and Considers His Words 119

PROVERBS 12:11 Meaningful Hard Work 125

PROVERBS 9:7-9 Be Wise and Accept Constructive Counsel 127

PROVERBS 11:16 The Enduring Honor of a Gracious Godly Person 131

PROVERBS 19:21 Human Plans Failing as God's Purpose Succeeds...133

PROVERBS 8:35-36 Finding Life...........................135

PROVERBS 12:25 Kind Words Are Healthy to Self and Others..138

PROVERBS 13:15 Hate What God Hates 140

PROVERBS 12:9 Living Within Our Means 142

PROVERBS 11:10-13 The Upright Bring Peace and Well-being While Wicked Sow Disorder, Corruption, and Moral Decline 144

Bibliography...150

INTRODUCTION The Meaning of Proverbs

Authorship

Solomon is attributed as the author at the introduction of three sections of the book of Proverbs. (Prov. 1:1; 10:1; 25:1) This would be in agreement with that Solomon "spoke three thousand proverbs, and his songs were one thousand and five." (1 Kings 4:32) There is very little doubt that many, if not all, of the proverbs in these three sections, must have been recorded during the reign of Solomon. Referring to himself, Solomon stated, "In addition to being a wise man, the Teacher also taught the people knowledge, and he pondered and made a thorough search in order to arrange many proverbs. The Teacher sought to find delightful words and to record accurate words of truth." – Eccles. 12:9-10.

Nonetheless, numerous arguments have been raised against crediting most of the proverbs to Solomon. Specific proverbs (Prov. 16:14; 19:12; 20:2; 25:3) have been mentioned as being critical, unfavorable, even disparaging to monarchs and therefore not from the time of Solomon. However, if we were to examine these proverbs closer, we would find, these proverbs do just the opposite in that they exalt kings. What they show is that the king should be given a measure of fear and respect because of the power that they possess. (See Prov. 24:21)

Some have argued that Solomon was a polygamist in the extreme and so, therefore, he would not have spoken of the husband-wife relationships in such a way as to suggest monogamy. (Prov. 5:15-19; 18:22; 19:13-14) However, those making such an argument are forgetting that polygamy was not supported or promoted but simply tolerated and controlled by the Mosaic Law. Moreover, it is likely that the vast majority of the Jews had monogamous marriages. Moreover, these critics tend to always look at the Bible as a book by man, a human book. Proverbs is inspired by God and its authors were moved along by the Holy Spirit. Therefore, what the Solomon wrote is actually what God said, not Solomon's opinion. Even so, from his views and beliefs and his own life-experiences Solomon may very well have come to his senses and appreciated the wisdom of God that he was moved speak and pen. – Compare Eccles. 2:8; 7:27-29.

The proverbs nor accredited to Solomon belonged to the sayings of other wise men (Agur and Lemuel) and one wise woman. (Prov. 22:17; 30:1; 31:1) We do not know the precise time when the proverbs were put in their final form. The final time indicator appearing in the book of Proverbs itself is a reference to King Hezekiah's reign. "These also are proverbs of Solomon which the men of Hezekiah king of Judah copied." (Prov. 25:1) So, it had to be during or shortly after the reign of Hezekiah when they were gathered in their final form. Hezekiah ruled about 715-686 B.C.E. Because of the repetition of certain proverbs, some have suggested that the book was assembled from various separate collections. - Compare 10:1 and 15:20; 10:2 and 11:4; 14:20 and 19:4; 16:2 and 21:2.

Historical Setting (Bible Background)

When Solomon, the tenth son of David and the second son of Bathsheba, became king of Israel in 1000 B.C.E., he prayed to God for "wisdom and knowledge that I may go out and come in before this people, for who can judge this, your great people." In response, God gave him "knowledge and wisdom" and "a wise and discerning heart." (2 Chron. 1:10-12; 1 Ki. 3:12; 4:30-31) As a result, Solomon "spoke three thousand proverbs, and his songs were one thousand and five." (1 Kings 4:32) This "wisdom, which God had put into his mind" is why some were recorded in the book of Proverbs. (1 Kings 10:23-24) Therefore, when we study these words of wisdom, we are really studying the wisdom of God. These proverbs are truths that will be applicable for an eternity.

"Solomon sat on the throne of Jehovah as king in place of David his father. And he prospered, and all Israel obeyed him." "And Jehovah made Solomon very great in the sight of all Israel and bestowed on him such royal majesty as had not been on any king before him in Israel." (1 Chron. 29:23, 25) It certainly was a time of "peace on all sides around him" and plenty, a time of great security. (1 Kings 4:20-25) Nevertheless, even then, because of human imperfection and our sinful nature, the Israelite people still had their personal problems and difficulties. It is completely understandable that the Jewish people would look to wise King Solomon to help them solve their problems. (1 Kings 3:16-28) As carried out the judgment of the many cases before him, Solomon uttered many proverbial sayings that fit the many life circumstances of the day. As they began to be compiled, this brief but powerful sayings would have been treasured by those seeking to live their lives according to God's Will.

Literary Form

The book of Proverbs is written in Hebrew poetic style, which consists of thought rhythm, employing parallelisms, the ideas of which are either similar (Prov. 11:25; 16:18; 18:15) or contrasting. (10:7, 30; 12:25; 13:25; 15:8) In the first section (1:1–9:18), they are composed of short discourses addressed from a father to a son or sons. This introduces the reader to the short, pithy sayings found in the remaining sections of the book. The final 22 verses of the book are written in acrostic, or alphabetic, style, a form of composition also used by David for a number of his psalms. – Psalm 9, 10, 25, 34, 37, 145.

Authenticity

The authors of the Greek New Testament are a testimony to the fact that the book of Proverbs is part of the inspired, inerrant Word of God. The apostle Peter (1 Pet. 4:18; 2 Pet. 2:22; Prov. 11:31 [LXX]; 26:11) and the disciple James (James 4:6; Prov. 3:34, LXX) referred to it, as did the apostle Paul when writing to the Corinthians (2 Cor. 8:21; Prov. 3:4, LXX), the book of Romans (Rom. 12:16, 20; Prov. 3:7; 25:21-22), and the Hebrews (Heb. 12:5, 6; Prov. 3:11-12). In addition, many parallel thoughts may be found in the New Testament. – Compare Prov. 3:7 with Rom. 12:16; Prov. 3:12 with Rev. 3:19; Prov. 24:21 with 1 Pet. 2:17; Prov. 25:6, 7 with Luke 14:7-11.

Purpose

Undeniably, so completely does the book of Proverbs cover every human need and situation that William Smith could state, "There is no relation in life which has not its appropriate instruction, no good or evil tendency without its proper incentive or correction. The human consciousness is everywhere brought into immediate relation with the Divine, ... and man walks as in the presence of his Maker and Judge ... Every type of humanity is found in this ancient book; and though sketched three thousand years ago, is still as true to nature as if now drawn from its living representative."[1]

The book itself gives the reader the purpose, "To know wisdom and discipline, to understand words of

---

[1] William Smith, *Smith's Dictionary of the Bible* (New York, NY: Hurd and Houghton, Cambridge Riverside Press, 1890), Vol. III, page 2616.

insight, to receive instruction in wise dealing, in righteousness, justice, and uprightness; to give shrewdness to the inexperienced, to the young man knowledge and thinking ability." (Prov. 1:2-4) "So you will walk in the way of the good men and keep to the paths of the righteous." – 2:20.

Place and Date of Writing

The greater part of the book of Proverbs was no doubt written down during the reign of Solomon (970–930 B.C.E.) before his falling away. Seeing that we are uncertain as to the identity of Agur and Lemuel, it is impossible to date their material. Considering that one of the collections was penned during the reign of Hezekiah (715–686 B.C.E.), it had to have been during or shortly after his reign that the book was collected in its final form. It would seem that the last two divisions were also collected under King Hezekiah's influence?

Interpreting Proverbs

A proverb is a short well-known pithy saying that expresses an obvious truth and often offers advice in a forceful way and is to the point, and frequently with an element of wit. Generally, the proverb will describe somebody or something with a word or phrase that is not meant to be taken literally. By means of a vivid comparison, proverbs express something about a person or thing. While we do have a whole book of Proverbs, they are found all throughout the Bible.

Isaiah 5:21 Updated American Standard Version (UASV)

[21] Woe to those who are wise in their own eyes,
and discerning in their own sight!

Proverbs have caused some difficulty in many churches because they are treated like absolutes or guarantees; if we do **A** we will get **B**. Proverbs are not to be applied in this sense in an imperfect world, with imperfect people. The best phrase that we can put before the proverb is "generally speaking." Let us look at Proverbs 22:6 as our example, it says, "train up a child in the way he should go; even when he is old he will not depart from it." (ESV) Let us look at an easy version of this, "direct your children onto the right path, and when they are older, they will not leave it." (NLT) Is this an absolute guarantee that, if I raise my children in the best way, when they get older they will not leave it? No. Let us place our phrase in front of it. 'Generally speaking,' if you direct your children onto the right path, and when they are older, they will not leave it.'

Again, we ask, is a proverb to be interpreted as a universal law? Is it as the law of the Medes and the Persians, which could never be overruled (Esther 8:8)? Is it to be interpreted absolutely, as the laws of thermodynamics, which describe what must always take place? It is apparent when reading proverbs that many of them seem to be less than absolute in their applicability. Let us look at a few more examples,

Proverbs 1:33 Updated American Standard Version (UASV)

[33] "But he who listens to me shall dwell securely
and he will live, without the dread of disaster."

Is it not true, even some of the most spiritual people we know, have suffered a lack of peace in war-torn countries (i.e., **have not** dwelled securely), or have had trouble in a bad neighborhood, as they fearfully walk to the store, or get in and out of their car, even walk out on their front porch? Was not Stephen of the first century a very spiritual Christian, and was he not martyred?

Proverbs 3:9-10 Updated American Standard Version (UASV)

⁹ Honor Jehovah with your wealth
  and with the firstfruits of all your produce;
¹⁰ then your barns will be filled with plenty,
  and your vats will be bursting with wine.

Have not many good Christians given much to the congregation out of their heart over the years, and suffered financial disaster during an economic downturn?

Proverbs 10:3-4 Updated American Standard Version (UASV)

³ Jehovah does not let the soul of the righteous go hungry,
  but he thrusts away the craving of the wicked.
⁴ A slack hand causes poverty,
  but the hand of the diligent makes rich.

Are there not poor Christians, who work hard at minimum wage jobs; while there are rich people, who have never worked a day in their life?

Proverbs 13:21 Updated American Standard Version (UASV)

²¹ Misfortune pursues sinners,
but the righteous are rewarded with good.[2]

Do we measure the righteous by who is the most blessed? Are all righteous people rich?

Proverbs 17:2 Updated American Standard Version (UASV)

² A servant who deals wisely will rule over a son who acts shamefully
  and will share in the inheritance among brothers.

Are there not wicked rich people?

---

[2] Or *prosperity*

It is obvious that none of these are absolutes. However, if we follow the rule and place "generally speaking" before the proverb, we will arrive at what the author meant. Generally speaking, all who listen to the principles of God, will have peace, untroubled by harm. Keeping physically clean contributes to good health. (Deuteronomy 23:12-13) God's servants must always speak the truth. (Ephesians 4:25) Sex before marriage, adultery, bestiality, incest, and homosexuality are all serious sins against God. – Leviticus 18:6; Romans 1:26, 27; 1 Corinthians 6:9-10.

Christians must avoid lying. (Pro. 6:16-19; Col. 3:9-10) They do not take part in any kind of gambling. (Eph. 5:3-5) In addition, Christians do not steal. Additionally, they do not knowingly buy property that they know to be stolen, nor do they take things without the owner's permission. (Ex. 20:15; Eph. 4:28) Christians have learned to control their anger, as uncontrolled anger can lead to acts of violence. (Gen. 4:5-8) God does not accept a person that is violent or even loves violence as his friend. (Psa. 11:5; Pro. 22:24-25) Christians do not take revenge or to return evil for the bad things that others might do to us. (Pro. 24:29; Rom. 12:17-21) There is nothing in the Bible that prohibits drinking alcoholic beverages. (Psa. 104:15; 1 Tim. 5:23) However, heavy drinking and drunkenness are condemned. (1 Cor. 5:11-13; 1 Tim. 3:8) A person, who consumes too much alcohol will more than likely ruin their health and upset their family. Moreover, it will decrease one's spiritual thinking ability, causing them to give into temptations. – Proverbs 23:20-21, 29-35.

The Hebrew word for "proverb" is *mashal*, and is believed to be from a root word, meaning, "to liken" or "compare." Psalm 49:12 says, "Man in his pomp [i.e., honor, fame, wealth] will not remain; **he is like** [or comparable to] the beasts that perish." This is certainly true, as many of the proverbs within Scripture make use of likenesses or comparisons. Milton Terry ads,

The same verb means also to rule, or have dominion, and some have sought to trace a logical connection between the two significations; but, more probably, as Gesenius suggests, two distinct and independent radicals have coalesced under this one form. The proverb proper will generally be found, in its ultimate analysis, to be a comparison or similitude. Thus, the saying, which became a proverb (*mashal*) in Israel, "Is Saul also among the prophets?" arose from his prophesying after the manner of the prophets with whom he came in contact (1 Sam. 10:10-12). The proverb used by Jesus in the synagogue of Nazareth, "Physician, heal thyself," is a condensed parable, as, indeed, it is there called (Luke 4:23), and it would be no difficult task to enlarge it into a parabolic narrative. Herein, also we may see how proverbs and parables came to be designated by the same word. The word *paroimia*, adage, byword, expresses more nearly the later idea commonly associated with the Hebrew *mashal*, and stands as its representative in the Septuagint. In the New Testament it is used in the sense of adage, or common byword, in 2 Peter 2:22, but in John's Gospel it denotes more especially an enigmatical discourse (John 10:6; John 16:15, 29). (Terry 1883, 329)

If the above were true, it would mean that, at times, we are talking about the sayings of a ruler, which means it would carry authority and power, or at least suggest superior wisdom. We do have a text that is consistent with this view, King Solomon "also uttered three thousand proverbs; and his songs were a thousand and five." – 1 Kings 4:32.

Amid the Israelites, there were widely held or regularly used expressions, which were packed with meaning on account of the situations that surrounded them. Mostly, these proverbial sayings were succinctly stated. (1 Sam. 10:12) However, not all of the proverbial sayings communicated correct views, and God took issue with them.

Ezekiel 12:22-23 (ESV)

²² "Son of man, what is this proverb that you have about the land of Israel, saying, 'The days grow long, and every vision comes to nothing'? ²³ Tell them therefore, 'Thus says the Lord God: I will put an end to this proverb, and they shall no more use it as a proverb in Israel.' But say to them, The days are near, and the fulfillment of every vision.

Ezekiel 18:2-3 (ESV)

² "What do you mean by repeating this proverb concerning the land of Israel, 'The fathers have eaten sour grapes, and the children's teeth are set on edge'? ³ As I live, declares the Lord God, this proverb shall no more be used by you in Israel.

Some of the proverbs turned into common expressions of mockery or disdain for certain people

Habakkuk 2:6 Updated American Standard Version (UASV)

⁶ Will not all these take up a **proverb** against him,
   Even mockery and insinuations against him, saying,
"Woe to him who increases what is not his'?
   For how long?
   And makes himself rich with loans?"

Here we have, more exactly the object of contempt, be it a person or something inanimate being referred to as "a proverbial." Hence, the Israelites were warned that if they failed to pay attention to God, obeying his commandments,

Deuteronomy 28:15

Updated American Standard Version (UASV)

[15] But it shall come to pass, if you will not listen to the voice of Jehovah your God, to observe to do all his commandments and his statutes which I command you this day, that all these curses shall come upon you, and overtake you.

Deuteronomy 28:37

Updated American Standard Version (UASV)

[37] And you will become an astonishment, a proverb, and a byword, among all the peoples where Jehovah will lead you away.

1 Kings 9:7

Updated American Standard Version (UASV)

[7] then I will cut off Israel from the land that I have given them, and the house that I have consecrated for my name I will cast out of my sight, and Israel will become a proverb and a byword among all peoples.

2 Chronicles 7:20

Updated American Standard Version (UASV)

[20] then I will pluck you up from my land that I have given you, and this house that I have consecrated for my name, I will cast out of my sight, and I will make it a proverb and a byword among all peoples.

Israel eventually did become a proverb and a byword [catch phrase] among the nations, as the following expressions show,

Psalm 44:13-15 Updated American Standard Version (UASV)

13 You make us a reproach to our neighbors,
 A scoffing and a derision to those around us.
14 You have made us a proverb[3] among the nations,
 a laughing stock among the peoples.
15 All day long my dishonor is before me,
 and shame has covered my face

Jeremiah 24:9 Lexham English Bible (LEB)

9 And I will make them as a terror, an evil to all the kingdoms of the earth, as a disgrace and a proverb, as a taunt and a curse, in all the places where I will drive them.

There were individuals, who became an object of scorn or a joke among the people, the subject among the drunkards,

Psalm 69:11-12 Updated American Standard Version (USV)

11 When I made sackcloth my clothing,
I became a proverb[4] to them.
12 Those who sit in the gate talk about me,
And I *am* the song of the drunkards.

11 When I made sackcloth my clothing,
 I became a byword to them.

12 Those who sit in the gate talk about me,

 And I am the song of the drunkards.

Job 17:6 Updated American Standard Version (UASV)

6 "But He has made me a proverb[5] of the people,
And I am one at whom men spit.

---

[3] Or object of scorn or a joke among the nations
[4] Or object of scorn
[5] Or object of scorn

As we can see from the above texts, to be a made a proverb of the people or of the nations, was to become an object of scorn, taking on a very low state in life.

While most proverbs are short pithy sayings, this is not always the case, as Isaiah chapter 14 contains a lengthier one. It compares the catastrophic result of the arrogance of the king of Babylon. With cutting, bitter mockery and derision, it piles scorn on the one who thought of himself as the "Shining morning star."

When the comparison or similitude contained in the proverb, was also rather unclear or puzzling, it could also be viewed as a riddle.

Psalm 78:2 Updated American Standard Version (UASV)

2 I will open my mouth in a parable;
I will utter riddles from of old,

An example of this can be found in the book of Ezekiel, where he made the following comparison,

Ezekiel 17:2-18 Updated American Standard Version (UASV)

2 "Son of man, propound a riddle and speak a parable to the house of Israel, 3 say, Thus says Jehovah God: A great eagle with great wings and long pinions, rich in plumage of many colors, came to Lebanon and took the top of the cedar. 4 He plucked off the topmost of its young twigs and carried it to a land of merchants and set it in a city of traders. 5 Then he took of the seed of the land and planted it in fertile soil.6 He placed it beside abundant waters; he set it like a willow, 6 and it sprouted and became a spreading vine, low in height with its branches turned toward him, yet its roots stayed under it. So it became a vine, produced branches, and sent out shoots.

---

6 Lit *a field of seed*

⁷ "And there was another great eagle with great wings and much plumage, and behold, this vine bent its roots toward him and shot forth its branches toward him from the bed where it was planted, that he might water it. ⁸ It had been planted in good soil[7] by abundant waters, that it might produce branches and bear fruit and become a noble vine.

⁹ "Say, Thus says Jehovah God: Will it thrive? Will he not pull up its roots and cut off its fruit, so that it withers, so that all its fresh sprouting leaves wither? It will not take a strong arm or many people to pull it from its roots. ¹⁰ Look, though it is planted, will it thrive? Will it not completely wither as soon as the east wind strikes it, wither on the bed where it sprouted?'"

¹¹ Then the word of Jehovah came to me, saying ¹² "Say now to the rebellious house, Do you not know what these things mean? Tell them, look, the king of Babylon came to Jerusalem, and took her king and her princes and brought them to him to Babylon. ¹³ And he took one of the royal offspring[8] and made a covenant with him, putting him under oath, and he took the chief men of the land, ¹⁴ that the kingdom might be humble and not lift itself up, and keep his covenant that it might stand. ¹⁵ But he rebelled against him by sending his ambassadors to Egypt, that they might give him horses and a large army. Will he succeed? Can one escape who does such things? Can he break the covenant and yet escape?

¹⁶ "As I live, declares the Lord God, surely in the place where the king dwells who made him king, whose oath he despised, and whose covenant with him he broke, in Babylon he shall die. ¹⁷ Pharaoh with his mighty army and great company will not help him in war, when mounds are cast up and siege walls built to cut off many lives ¹⁸ He

---

[7] Lit *field*
[8] Lit *seed*

despised the oath in breaking the covenant, and look, he gave his hand and did all these things; he shall not escape.

The Case of Job

What we have covered thus far will help us understand one of the most complex books of the Bible, the book of Job.

Job was a "blameless and upright man, who fears God and turns away from evil." Job was living the happy life; he had seven sons and the daughters. He was a wealthy landowner. "He possessed 7,000 sheep, 3,000 camels, 500 yoke of oxen, and 500 female donkeys, and very many servants, so that this man was the greatest of all the people of the east." (1:3) Even so, he is not a materialistic person; he was only following a proverb like the above, 'if you work hard, your efforts will be blessed.'

Job 1:13-19; 2:7-8 Updated American Standard Version (UASV)

13 Now there was a day when his sons and daughters were eating and drinking wine in the house of their oldest brother, 14 and a messenger came to Job and said, "The oxen were plowing and the donkeys feeding beside them, 15 and the Sabeans attacked[9] and took them and struck down the servants with the edge of the sword, and I alone have escaped to tell you."16 While he was yet speaking, there came another and said, "The fire of God fell from heaven and burned up the sheep and the servants and consumed them, and I alone have escaped to tell you." 17 While he was yet speaking, there came another and said, "The Chaldeans formed three groups and made a raid on the camels and took them and struck down the servants with the edge of the sword, and I alone have escaped to tell you." 18 While he was yet speaking, there

---

[9] Lit *fell upon*

came another and said, "Your sons and daughters were eating and drinking wine in the house of their oldest brother, [19] and behold, a great wind came across the wilderness and struck the four corners of the house, and it fell upon the young people, and they are dead, and I alone have escaped to tell you."

[7] So Satan went out from the presence of Jehovah, and he inflicted Job with loathsome skin sores from the sole of his foot up to the crown of his head. [8] And he took for himself a potsherd with which to scrape himself, and he sat in the midst of the ashes.

The Comforters

Job 4:7-8 Updated American Standard Version (UASV)

[7] "Remember: who that was innocent ever perished?
Or where were the upright cut off?
[8] As I have seen, those who plow iniquity
and sow trouble reap the same.

Eliphaz in an attempt at dealing with Job's atrocities assumes Job's tragedies are a result of his own actions. Eliphaz has reasoned wrong by taking a proverb and making it an absolute. In essence, he asks Job, 'do those that are innocent die? When have those that live a righteous life been destroyed?' Eliphaz goes on by saying, 'my experience suggests that it is those who are doing wrong and entertain bad that will get back what they gave out.' In other words, Eliphaz is assuming that only the wicked reap bad times.

Job 5:15 Updated American Standard Version (UASV)

[15] But he saves from the sword of their mouth
and the poor from the hand of the mighty.

Eliphaz again assumes that Job is at fault. Eliphaz is assuming that it was Job's great riches, which were ill gotten, and this is why he is suffering. Is Eliphaz's statement wrong in and of itself? No, God does rescue the poor from the oppressive, by their following his counsel on the right way to live. However, this is no absolute; saying all who live by God's will and purposes will never be mistreated. Moreover, the whole idea is misplaced, in that maybe Job is the rich oppressor and this is his punishment from God.

Job 8:3-6 Updated American Standard Version (UASV)

[3] Does God pervert justice?
   Or does the Almighty pervert the right?
[4] If your sons have sinned against him,
   he has delivered them into the hand of their transgression.
[5] If you will seek God
   and plead with the Almighty for mercy,
[6] if you are pure and upright,
   surely then he will rouse himself for you
   and restore your rightful place.[10]

Bildad too is stating true statements, but in absolute terms that are misplaced when it comes to Job or anyone. Certainly, God does not pervert justice. Therefore, Bildad is right on that, but his application and understanding are what is twisted, as he assumes that children died because they had sinned, and justice was being meted out to them. Again, in verse 5-6, we have a true thought, in that if one is in an impure state, and turns to God with pleads, he will restore them. However, in verses 5-6, Bildad is assuming that Job is unrighteous because he sees that proverb as an absolute.

As can be seen from the above, one must be aware that proverbs are not absolutes, but are general truths. True enough, there are likely a couple of exceptions to this

---

[10] I.e., *habitation*

rule, but that would not negate this rule, and approach of correct interpretation of proverbs.

Rules for Interpreting Proverbs

A proverb can be a simile, a metaphor, a parable, even an allegory. Therefore, we must first ascertain which of these fits our proverb under consideration. For example, Proverbs 5:15-18 is an allegory, which "depicts a model of chastity for the godly husband and wife through the figure of cool, fresh flowing water, so precious in an arid country. What a beautiful way to portray the never-ending love relationship of a husband for his wife." (Goldberg 2000, 20)

If we are to interpret correctly the proverbs found all through Scripture, we have to be critical and practical combined with intelligence and good judgment, i.e., wise and shrewd. Some proverbs are only just straightforward facts; "Even a child makes himself known by his acts, by whether his conduct is pure and upright." (Pro 20:15) Have our children's "actions" shown them to be "pure and upright" or careless and irresponsible?

Then again, some proverbs are simple principles, teachings, rules, guidelines, instructions and truisms of a good and righteous life, or warnings against sin, which is understandable to anyone, such as Proverbs 3:5, "Trust in Jehovah with all your heart and do not lean on your own understanding." Another example would be Proverbs 4:14, "Do not go where evil people go. Do not follow the example of the wicked." Then again, there are proverbs, which demand that we slow down and critically examine then, like Proverbs 25:27, "It is not good to eat much honey, Nor is it glory to search out one's own glory." Verse 27b literally reads, "The seeking of their glory is glory." Most take 27b, as saying the proud can never get enough glory. In fact, they will even seek the glory that belongs to others, even the glory that rightfully belongs to God. However, Duane A. Garrett writes,

> With minor emending, however, it can be translated, "But seeking out difficult things is glorious."[11] While this creates a surprising response to line a, it looks back to v. 2 in the same way that line a looks back to v. 16. The chiastic structure of the whole is as follows: glory (v. 2)/ honey (v. 16)/honey (v. 27a)/glory (v. 27b).[12] While an excess of sweets does no one good, the wise never can get enough of unraveling the riddles of the sages. (Garrett 1993, 209)

Of the many proverbs found within Scripture, most need some contemplation, to come away with what the author meant by the words that he used; others were designed to puzzle but can be investigated and explained with the treasure house of Bible study tools available to us today. Along with these tools is the context that a proverb lies within; therefore, the immediate context is where one should begin.

In addition, we need to consider the poetic parallelisms. The identical and the complete or exact opposite parallelisms, especially, are modified; by way of the similarities and contrasts they provide, which put forward their own meaning from within. For example, Proverbs 11:25, which reads, "The generous man will be fat [prosperous], and he who waters will himself be

---

[11] Reading וְחֵקֶר כְּבֵדִים כָּבוֹד. See G. E. Bryce, "Another Wisdom 'Book' in Proverbs," *JBL* 91 (1972): 145–57. The word כְּבֵדִים is here short for דְּבָרִים כְּבֵדִים ("difficult things").

[12] Ibid., 153. More precisely the Hebrew chiasmus shows the following word pairs:

חקר ´´ כבד (v. 2) and חקר ´´ כבד (v. 27b)
דבש ´´ אכל (v. 16a) and אכל ´´ דבש (v. 27a).

watered." If we look at the second half of the parallelism, we will see that it is a metaphorical illustration of the rather hard to understand feeling or opinion of the first half. Looking at another, we see Proverbs 12:24, which reads, "The hand of the diligent will rule, But the slack [hand] will be put to forced labor." Again, we are dealing with a metaphor, in which the contrast makes transparent.

Milton brings us back to what was spoken of at the outset, but bears repeating yet again; we need "to guard us against construing all proverbs as universal propositions. Proverbs 16:7, expresses a great truth: 'When Jehovah delights in the ways of a man he makes even his enemies be at peace with him.' But there have been many exceptions to this statement, and many cases to which it could apply only with considerable modification. Such, to some extent, have been all cases of persecution for righteousness' sake. So, too, with verse 13 of the same chapter: "Delight of kings are lips of righteousness, and him that speaks right things he will love." The annals of human history show that this has not always been true, and yet the most impious kings understand the value of upright counselors." (Terry 1883, 332-3) Here again, it is best to put the phrase, "generally speaking" before these proverbs that are not universal laws.

REVIEW QUESTIONS Introduction

- What wisdom is to be found in the book of Proverbs?
- Why was Solomon's time an appropriate one in which to provide the divine guidance in Proverbs?
- How did Proverbs come to be compiled?
- Who originated the bulk of the proverbs?
- When was Proverbs written and compiled?
- What is a proverb, and why is the Hebrew title of the book fitting?
- What should be noted about the style of Proverbs?

- How does the use made of Proverbs by the early Christians testify to its authenticity?
- How do you interpret the genre of proverbs?

PROVERBS 10:11 Life Giving Wisdom or Life Destroying Ignorance

Proverbs 10:11 Updated American Standard Version (UASV)

¹¹ The mouth of the righteous is a fountain of life,
   but the mouth of the wicked conceals violence.

The mouth of the righteous is a fountain of life: Words from the mouth of the righteous (good, honest, upright person) refers to words and thoughts, which can heal. They can refresh, enliven, and inspire a person. They can also lead to eternal life. **The fountain of life** reminds us of the **tree of life** back in 3:18.

Wisdom is "a fountain of life to one who has it," in that wisdom will supply us with that which we require, not only to enjoy our present life but also to obtain eternal life (John 3:16; 17:3), that is, accurate knowledge of God and the insight and good sense to be obedient to his commands. – Proverbs 3:18; 16:22.

but the mouth of the wicked conceals violence: Words from the mouth of the wicked (bad, dishonest, unrighteous, fallen person) can hurt. They can depress, destroy, discourage, damage, and dishearten a person. They can tear him down. They can also lead to eternal destruction, as Paul spoke of in 2 Thessalonians 1:9.

If our words are to contain life-giving wisdom instead of life-destroying ignorance, we must meditate on the knowledge of God. (2:5) We must empty our mind of the old way of thinking, removing the old person, to make room for our new way of thinking, taking on the mind of Christ. Then, we must give time for the new biblical worldview to filter in by our meditation on God's Word. If we do not keep our thoughts growing in the Word of God, changing our old fleshly worldview, they become stagnant and stale.

If we allow all of the worldly waste and satanic propaganda to fill our mind, we will have no room for godly thinking. Therefore, it is with the mind as it is with the bountiful source of well water: if we are always dipping the water out of the well, it goes dry. However, if we never dip the water out it becomes stale. There is a time for dipping the water out, there is a time for seeping the water in. There is the right time to speak and a perfect time to hold back our words, a time to ponder and a time to share our words, a time to reason and reflect and a time to share the words of what you have been thinking. If we are to share first, we must receive. We must take in life-saving knowledge before we can give out life-saving knowledge. We must fill our minds inspired, inerrant Word before we can unload the treasures of the knowledge of God and we must unload before we can fill again. It is an ongoing process of both getting and giving, not just one or the other. We need to keep the waters of biblical truth running into our minds, meditatively through our mind, and out of our mouths.

Review Questions (10:11) Words from the mouth of the **righteous** can do what? Words from the mouth of the **wicked** can do what?

PROVERBS 3:5-6 Make Personal Decisions Wisely

Proverbs 3:5-6 Updated American Standard Version (UASV)

⁵ Trust in Jehovah with all your heart,
  and do not lean on your own understanding.
⁶ In all your ways acknowledge him,
  and he will make straight your paths.

Trust in Jehovah with all your heart: **Trust** means to rely on, depend on, have confidence in, to have a firm belief in the reliability, truth, ability, or strength of someone, and, in this case, Jehovah God. (2 Ki 18:5; 18:30; Ps 22:10; Isa 36:15; Jer. 28:15; 29:31) When we trust in God, this means that we know that he is our only true source of wisdom, strength, and power in everything that we think, feel, or do; therefore, we give him our complete trust. With all your **heart** means with all your mind, the element of a person that enables them to be aware of their Creator, the world and their experiences, to think, and to feel; the full force of the mental faculty of consciousness and thought, with no reservation.

And do not lean on your own understanding: **Lean on** renders a word (Heb. *šā·ʿăn*) meaning to lean upon oneself or support oneself. **Understanding** (Heb. *tᵉḇû·nā(h)*) is the ability to see how the parts or aspects of something are connected to one another. One who possesses understanding can see the big picture (comprehending the entire matter) and not just the isolated facts. In all your ways acknowledge him: **Your ways** are a reference to everything that you do. **Acknowledge him** is to know him, to have taken in knowledge and information about him, to have a personal intimate acquaintance with him, to be aware of him. Here in this context, knowing God goes beyond some intellectual awareness that he exists but rather accepting him for who he is and allowing him to guide and direct our lives.

And he will make straight your paths: **Make straight** renders a verb (Heb. *yā·šār*) that means to smooth out, make level, or remove the barriers to prepare a path, with a focus of our never wandering or turning from a course, inferring that we say the course with purpose or ease. In this context, it can refer to our life and the different moral choices that we will have to make.

Certainly, there is not another person that we could ever trust more than Jehovah God himself. If we are trusting Jehovah with all of our heart, this means that we completely surrender ourselves to him. Imagine that we were on a safari in Africa when the vehicle breaks down, and we are now being led by a guide through grasslands, scrub, or open woodlands, a 50-mile trek back to safety. Would we offer him our advice at every turn, question his decision, complain to any who might listen? No, we would give this guide our complete trust, because he is the expert and our life depend up his decisions. Jehovah God has given us his word, as a guide through this difficult part of human history. He is the expert, and our everlasting life depends upon him. Abraham entered into a lifelong journey of 100 years of traveling with Jehovah God as his guide, and the lands he traveled were far more dangerous than some African safari mishap. Abraham became the father of true faith and trust.

However, when it says **do not lean on your own understanding**, does this mean that we cannot think for ourselves? No, it is Jehovah God himself, who gave man the capacity to think and reason, which he expects us to use them wisely, to serve and worship him. Verse 5 is contrasting our thinking ability with the of Jehovah, in which case if what we think, feel, and believe is not in harmony with his, we are to go with his direction. In other words, in that case, his thinking would guide our own. (Isa. 30:21) If we are a serious student of God's Word, over time, we will become permeated with his way of thinking, and our decisions will reflect this.

Verse 6 is another if you do **(A)** you will get **(B)** situation. If we remember to trust Jehovah **(A)**, he will make our paths straight **(B)**. First, making our paths straight means that he will make our lives easier, as it is easier to follow a straight path. Of course, generally, if we completely trust Jehovah, life will be much easier, as we will avoid many pitfalls. However, life in an imperfect world, full of imperfect people, there is bound to be some difficulties. Nevertheless, we can know that our direction and purpose will always be straight.

Review Questions (3:5-6) Why should we make personal decisions wisely?

PROVERBS 1:7 The Beginning of Knowledge

Proverbs 1:7 Updated American Standard Version (UASV)

7 The fear of Jehovah is the beginning of knowledge;
 fools despise wisdom and instruction.

"The fear of Jehovah" is the repeated theme of wisdom found in the book of Proverbs.[13] One who fears Jehovah, he has the qualities of humility (15:33; 22:4), wisdom (1:7), possessing faithfulness and Godly love (16:6), and a concern for his relationship with God (2:5; 9:10). In the book of Proverbs, fear of Jehovah is related to faith in God that is constantly seeking understanding.[14] In what way is "the fear of Jehovah" "the beginning of knowledge" and 'the beginning of wisdom'? (9:10) If we did not have a fear of Jehovah (i.e., **not a** morbid dread of him but rather a profound reverence and awe in the presence of such an all-powerful person), we would have no knowledge, for the Father is the Creator of all things and the Author of the Spirit-inspired Scriptures. Therefore, we need to give Jehovah the proper place in our life. Life is from the Father, and life is, of course, indispensable for our having any knowledge.

Thus, on the threshold of this treasure house of wisdom, we are presented with one of the sharp contrasts with which the book abounds. There is no true knowledge apart from the fear of Jehovah. Again, the fear of Jehovah is not some morbid fear, but a reverence and fear of

---

[13] (cf. 1:29; 2:5; 9:10; 10:27; 14:26, 27; 15:16, 33; 16:6; 19:23; 22:4; 23:17)

[14] Leo G. Perdue, *Wisdom & Creation: The Theology of Wisdom Literature* (Nashville: Abingdon, 1994), p. 79.

displeasing him because of the love one has for him. All those making insincere claims to the name, and ignores him, is but foolish. It is well for all of to bear this in mind when meeting the difficulties of Satan's world. Many of the higher educated have cast to the winds the fear of Jehovah and ruled him out of his own creation. Thinking that they are all wise, they have become the fool.

The gift of life comes from Jehovah, the loss of perfect life was at the hands of rebellious man, and the restoration to everlasting life is an underserved kindness shown to man, from his Creator. Without life, there would be no knowledge. (Ps. 36:9; Ac 17:25, 28) The fact that God is the Creator of every living thing means that we need to have a better understanding of him, not the other way around. (Ps. 19:1-2; Rev. 4:11) Aside from the opportunity at everlasting life, God has given us his Word, the Bible, which "is profitable for teaching, for reproof, for correction, for training in righteousness, in order that the person of God may be competent, equipped for every good work." (2 Tim. 3:16-17) Therefore, the knowledge that is to be desired most is to be found with our heavenly Father, and if it is our desire to find the very knowledge of God, we must have a reverential fear of him.

The apostle Paul tells us, "Where is the wise man? Where is the scribe? Where is the debater of this age? Has not God made foolish the wisdom of the world?" (1 Cor. 1:20) Anyone who lacks the fear of Jehovah, even the wisest man who has ever lived, he will end up drawing wrong conclusions from what he believes to be known facts and end up being 'a fool.' The fear of Jehovah means that we dedicate our entire life of Godly devotion to the Father. The unbeliever may come to some basic truths about life, as he too is the product of being in the image of God (meaning his intellect comes from the Creator); however, he will never come to have the true or ultimate knowledge until he has a profound reverence and awe in the presence of such an all-powerful person, as Jehovah God.

Review Question (1:7) In what way is the fear of Jehovah "the beginning of knowledge" and "the start of wisdom"?

PROVERBS 4:18-19 Mental Darkness

Proverbs 4:18-19 Updated American Standard Version (UASV)

[18] But the path of the righteous is like the light of dawn,
   which shines brighter and brighter until full day.
[19] The way of the wicked is like deep darkness;
   they do not know over what they stumble.

But the path of the righteous is like the light of dawn: The conjunction **but** shows us that verse 18 and 19 will be contrasting the righteous person with the wicked person. The path of the righteous refers to the life course of the upright person, the blameless person. **Blameless**: (Heb. *tam, tamim*; Gr. *amomos, amometos*) means "perfect, blameless, sincerity, entire, whole, complete, and full." Of course, Noah, Jacob, and Job were said to be blameless and they were not literally perfect. When used of imperfect humans, the terms are relative, not absolute. However, if we are *fully* committed to following, a life course based on God's will and purposes, fully living by his laws, repent when we fall short, he will credit us righteousness. – Gen. 6:6; 25:27; Job 9:20-22l Ps. 119:1; Pro. 11:20; Phil 2:15; 1 Thess. 5:23.

The path of the righteous is **like** ... is a simile. **Similes** are normally introduced with the word "like" or "as." They compare two things that are very different, highlighting something these two things have in common. "He is **like** a tree planted by streams of water ..." (Psalm 1:3) In this simile, the **path of righteousness** is being compared to **the light of dawn**. What is the commonality between the two? **Dawn** occurs **before sunrise before** the top of the Sun reaches the horizon. So, the path of righteousness (life course of a blameless upright believer) is being compared rising sunlight, meaning the way in which they are to go is made clear, so they can be aware of the unseen dangers.

Which shines brighter and brighter until full day: The path or life course of the believer is one where there is increased light, just as the sunlight of dawn pulls the righteous one out of the darkness and into the light of the **full day.**

The way of the wicked is like deep darkness: This too is a simile, as it is introduced with the word "like." The way of the wicked is being compared to deep darkness. The deep darkness ($^{a}p\bar{e}\cdot l\bar{a}(h)$) spoken of here is mental darkness, not literal physical darkness. What is the commonality between the two? Like deep darkness, the wicked are in mental darkness in that they cannot see any light whatsoever. Mental darkness is a sort of mental blindness where one sees what others see and even understands the meaning, but their mind is beyond repentance, unreceptive, closed, so they see it as foolish. They are in darkness mentally.

The apostle Paul warns the reader at 2 Corinthians 4:4, "the god of this world [Satan] has blinded the minds of the unbelievers, to keep them from seeing the light of the gospel of the glory of Christ, who is the image of God." The apostle John says of Jesus Christ, "In him was life, and the life was the light of men. And the light shines in the darkness, and the darkness has not overpowered it." (John 1:4-5) However, even the light of the truth cannot penetrate the mental darkness of some.

They do not know over what they stumble: When you are in mental darkness, you are so blinded by your closed heart and mind, you cannot even see what is making you stumble. The Hebrew verb **stumble** (Heb. $k\bar{a}\cdot\check{s}\check{a}l$) means to walk blindly. In this context, it refers to a wicked, evil, person who basks in their willful ignorance (darkness).

A believer can pass from death to life by choosing Christ. However, he can also pass from life to death if he stumbles to the point of spiritual shipwreck. There are times when these ones can be recovered. (Gal 6:1) However, if he rejects the help from spiritual leaders within the congregation because his heart has grown callused, he can go to the point of being **beyond repentance**. He would come to the point of having no desire to be restored. (Heb. 6:4-8; 10:26-29) The wicked, foolish ones are beyond repentance and refuse to be corrected by Wisdom; therefore, **they shall eat the fruit of their way** (1:31), namely, suffer the consequences of their conduct. These ones have thrown their faith to the wind and have rejected God and have moved over to the point of being **beyond repentance**. Truly wicked ones will not change their ways, as they are in mental darkness, beyond repentance, unable to see any light whatsoever, and are blinded by the god of this wicked age. (2 Cor. 4:3-4) However, we can rescue the young one, who may fall prey to their seductive ways.

The contrast is all too clear, as the path of the righteous is one that grows brighter throughout his or her life, everything becoming clearer. On the other hand, the way of the wicked is so dark that they cannot even see what causes them to stumble. Those on the path of righteousness possess moral insight that adds joy to their life, while the way of the wicked possesses ignorance that leads to unhappiness. The objective of Solomon here is that he wants to whet the appetite of his sons for wisdom and insight, knowing the result will be that their actions will come thereafter.

PROVERBS 10:22 Enough Is Enough

Proverbs 10:22 Updated American Standard Version (UASV)

22 The blessing of Jehovah, it makes rich,
and he adds no sorrow to it.

The blessing of Jehovah makes rich: When we talk about the **blessing** of God, it is referring to the goodness and the kindness that he bestows upon his people. The emphasis here is on the good things that happen and come to those who heed the words of the Wise One. The Hebrew third-person pronoun (*hi*), which is rendered **it** was added by the author here for emphasis, referring back to where all the good things (blessings) come from, namely, Jehovah.

The Hebrew verb (*ashar*) means simply to be or become rich or wealthy. This is relative to the context. **Rich** here in this context is a contrast of one who has the basic needs of life over one who does not. If you have never lived on both sides of the poverty line, you will have a difficult time visualizing how a person who does not have enough income to acquire the bare necessities of life for their family can see a neighbor who has such basics as being rich. Riches (having basic necessities of life) are the result of hard work and poverty (not having bare necessities) is brought on by laziness. The bare necessities of life are food, clothing, shelter, and health.

and he adds no sorrow to it: If and when we ever gain a measure of wealth or riches because we have truly lived by the rules, principles, and moral values, ethics found in God's Word, it will be a blessing to us and others, as there will be no love of money involved. Many times, the wealthy unbelievers have sorrows over their riches because they have gained it or tries to maintain it unscrupulously, through dishonesty, or deceit. If this is not the case, the sorrows come from being fraught with tax problems, legal issues, and, of course, everyone now wants to be their friend. This is largely not the case with one who is living a just life and applying the words of the Wise One.

God blesses those who have a righteous standing before him (an approved condition) by protecting them, prospering their biblically based decisions, guiding them in the way that they should go, giving them success in the things they attempt, and supplying them with the basic needs, with a beneficial outcome for them.

PROVERBS 12:18 Do Your Words Stab or Heal?

Proverbs 12:18 Updated American Standard Version (UASV)

¹⁸ There is one whose rash words are like sword thrusts,
  but the tongue of the wise brings healing.

There is one whose rash words are like sword thrusts: The Hebrew expression here that is rendered **there is** (*yesh*) denotes the existence of someone, and in this case, one whose words are **rash**, which refers to words that are spoken too quickly without careful consideration of the possible consequences; impetuously. Such words can seem like (Heb. *chereb madqarah*) **sword thrusts**, which are quick jabs that are piercing motions, stabbing made with a sword, which cause serious wounds and injuries. While the language is figurative, the pain caused by rash words are very real.

but the tongue of the wise brings healing: Once more, as was true in verses 11, 13, 18, 20, 21, and in 31 in chapter 10, we have a part of the body (tongue, mouth, lips) being used figuratively with reference to the speech or words of good people. While the rash words of the thoughtless one can cause serious mental, emotional, spiritual, and even physical pain, the well-chosen, well thought out words of the wise or wise words can heal or restore the damage caused by the thoughtless one. Healing is the mental, emotional, spiritual, and even physical pain that is restored to health or a sound state.

The thoughtless fool with his rash or reckless words hurts others, but the wise person or the person using wise words, which are carefully chosen, well thought out can heal the person who is suffering from such thoughtless ones and their rash words. Even though we may see the one using rash words as thoughtless or a fool, it might not necessarily be intentional, for it is more of one who speaks too quickly without careful consideration of the other person and the possible consequences. While there may be no malice on the thoughtless one the damage to the other is like a sword thrust causing much emotional damage.

The wise person or a person with wise words may undo some of the damage afterward with his well-chosen words, to bring healing to the wounds. This person with his wise words can do more than heal the damage done but can prepare the other with the wisdom of rational thinking. Proverbs 23:7 tells us, "For as he thinketh in his heart, so is he." In other words, nothing anyone says can cause us emotional damage, it is what we think about what they say that causes the damage. If we can rationally perceive the truth, dismissing the irrational words, there is no emotional; damage being done.

PROVERBS 13:20 The Powerful Effect of Friends

Proverbs 13:20 Updated American Standard Version (UASV)

²⁰ He who walks with wise men will be wise,
  but the companion of fools will suffer harm.

He who walks with wise men will be wise: Walk: (Heb. *halak*) **in integrity** (Heb. *tōm*) a state of blamelessness being free of guilt. (Prov. 2:7) In the Bible, the expression "to walk" is figurative and illustrative and can mean to follow a certain course of action, as "Noah walked with God." (Gen. 6:9; 5:22) Those who walk with God follow the life course outlined by God's Word and will find his favor, that is, be pleasing to him. Pursuing such a life-course makes you different from most of the unbelievers. The Greek New Testament uses the same illustrative expression, contrasting two different courses of action sought by one before and after becoming a servant of God. (Eph. 2:2, 10; 4:17; 5:2) Similarly "running" is also used to symbolize a course of action. (1 Pet. 4:4) God tells us that the prophets in Judah "ran" though he did not send them, yet they took the prophetic course, that is, prophesied falsely. (Jer. 23:21) Paul gives us a visual picture of the Christian course in terms of "running." He compares it to a race that a person must run, while also obeying the rules of the race if they are to win the prize. – 1 Cor. 9:24; Gal. 2:2; 5:7.

Wisdom: (Heb. *chokmah*) is sound judgment, based on knowledge and understanding. It is the balanced application of that knowledge to answer difficulties, achieve objectives, sidestep or ward off dangers, not to mention helping others to accomplish the same. The wise person is often contrasted with the foolishness or stupid person. (Deut. 32:6; Prov. 11:29; Eccles. 6:8) The **wise** person (Heb. *chakam*) is one who is shrewd, as he has the ability to understand and discern, so he would be a trusted guide or advisor.

but the companion of fools will suffer harm: The **companion** (Heb. *raah*) is a friend or an associate of someone and, in this case, it is a friend who associates with a foolish person who does stupid things. **Fools**: (Heb. *kesîl*) hate knowledge as they lack good judgment. Their character is stupidity, rudeness, that is, one who completely lacks understanding, who is rebellious in his ways. (Prov. 1:22) **Foolishness**: (Heb. *ivveleth*) The foolishness of the foolish one, who has the trait of acting stupidly or rashly because he is devoid of wisdom or understanding, the Hebrew noun focusing on the evil behaviors which occur in this state. **Suffer harm** is an expression referring to physical or emotional pain.

Who are the **fools** with whom a wise person should have no associations? The fool is not simply just one who lacks knowledge but are ones who are unaware of moral truth, they are godless persons. This proverb is talking about more than mere casual contact with a foolish person. It is talking about a person with whom one spends a lot of time and shared experiences. What a powerful effect our friends, companions, and associates can have on our thoughts, our likes, and our dislikes! There is no denying the damage a bad companionship can bring. This can be for the better or it can be for the worse. As line one shows, good friends, wise friends can be real assistance in our continuing our walk with God. The implication here of **walking** with a wise person implies a close connection, who has a molding effect for good.

PROVERBS 9:4-6 Leaving Your Old Ways for the Ways of Wisdom

Proverbs 9:4-6 Updated American Standard Version (UASV)

4 "Whoever is simple,[15] let him turn in here!"
   As for him who is in want of heart,[16] she says to him,
5 "Come, eat of my bread
   and drink of the wine I have mixed.
6 Leave your simple ways,[17] and live,
   and walk in the way of understanding."

"Whoever is simple, let him turn in here!": The **simple** (Heb. *pethi*) referred to hear are the inexperienced, the lowly, humble of God's people. Wisdom's asking these ones of little education, who were scorned and disdained by the elite to **turn in here** [her house], to share a feast with her. While Wisdom's invitation to share a meal that she has prepared is the intended meaning, but the sense here is that these ones need to acquire wisdom and the benefits that it will bring.

When the Son of God came to the earth, he did not take the good news to the elite of the Jewish people, the wealthy, the Jewish religious leaders. We are told at Luke 4:16-21, "and he **[Jesus]** stood up to read. And the scroll of the prophet Isaiah was given to him. And he unrolled the scroll and found the place where it was written, 'The Spirit of the Lord is upon me, because he has anointed me to proclaim good news **to the poor**. He has sent me to proclaim release to **the captives** and recovering of sight to **the blind**, to set **free those who are oppressed**, to proclaim

---

[15] I.e. *inexperienced*
[16] I.e. *lacking good sense*
[17] I.e. *inexperience*

the favorable year of the Lord.' And he rolled up the scroll and gave it back to the attendant and sat down; and the eyes of all in the synagogue were fixed on him. And he began to say to them, 'Today **this Scripture has been fulfilled in your hearing.'"**

Yes, Jesus came to bring the good news of the kingdom, to free them from the Jewish religious leaders and those of noble birth, who were oppressing them. The apostle Paul told the Corinthians Christians similarly. He wrote, "For consider your calling, brothers, that there were **not many wise** according to the flesh [not wise according to human standards], **not** many **mighty, not** many **noble;** but **God has chosen the foolish** things of the world to shame the wise, and God has **chosen the weak** things of the world to shame the things which are strong, and the **insignificant** things [implying a lack of noble descent; inferior] of the world and **the despised** God has chosen, the things that are not, so that he might bring to nothing the things that are." – 1 Corinthians 1:26-29.

From the very start of Christianity, those who were chosen and those who were attracted to this new faith was primarily the lowly, humble people. The twelve apostles of Jesus Christ, the foundation of Christianity, were not selected from the elite of the Jewish religious leaders: the educated scribes and Pharisees. (Ephesians 2:20) Rather, they were from the working class who performs manual labor for very little wages, having the very basic education needed, four being fishermen by trade. (Matthew 4:18-22; 10:2-3) These men were viewed by the elite religious leaders as "uneducated[18] and untrained men." Young's Literal Translation (YLT) has "unlettered," that is, not educated in the rabbinic schools; not meaning illiterate. (Acts 4:13) These so-called "lettered" highly educated scribes and Pharisees talked down to, disparaged,

---

[18] Or *unlettered* (YLT) that is, not educated in the rabbinic schools; not meaning illiterate.

denigrated the long-awaited Messiah, scornful and disdainful of his teachings and his followers.

As for him who is in want of heart, she says to him: An inexperienced person is newly learning as to the ways of Wisdom. Because he is inexperienced, this one may be "in want of heart," as Solomon expresses it. The Hebrew (*chaser leb*) is rendered (interpreted) as "lacks sense" in other translations. (ESV, LEB, CSB) Again, this is an inexperienced person, who is lacking good sense and wisdom, lacking good judgment or discernment in that they are newly learning the ways of Wisdom. This one's motives need not necessarily be bad and it will take some time to bring one's heart in the ways of Wisdom. This involves bringing this inexperienced one, the new one' thoughts, desires, affections, emotions, and goals in life into harmony with the will and purposes of God. When someone has put on the new person, has acquired a biblical worldview, has the mind of Christ, they have molded the inner person in a godly way, "getting heart." – Proverbs 19:8.

"Come, eat of my bread: The Hebrew word for bread (*lechem*) can be used in a general sense for food.

and drink of the wine I have mixed: Here, again, mixed wine may refer to the practice of diluting wine with water. The Jewish people did not find undiluted wine as being tasteful. The wine on Passover was mixed with three parts water and one-part wine. Then, again, there was also the practice of mixing spices into the wine to give it a variety of flavors. Or, it could be that wisdom did both of these.

Leave your simple ways, and live: These inexperienced ones need to leave behind their foolish ways, quit associating with ignorant ones who reject the ways of Wisdom. **And live** (Heb. *chayah*) is giving one's former life with these foolish ones.

and walk in the way of understanding.": In the Hebrew walking (*ashar*) can be following a life course and the sense of the word here is behavior, to now live or behave in the way of Wisdom. **Understanding** (Heb. *binah*) is the ability to see how the parts or aspects of something are connected to one another. One who possesses understanding can see the big picture (the entire matter) and not just the isolated facts.

Lady Wisdom has sent out her servant girls to town, to invite everyone, who is able to hear her voice. She is especially looking for those that lack understanding or are simply confused as to the life that is before them, these being the inexperienced ones. These ones are being offered a chance at a different kind of life than they had previously known. The wisdom found within God's Word is able to help man in his imperfection, to make the choices that he would have made under perfection. Simply put, the simple (inexperienced; lacking good sense) are invited to the feast, so that they can become wise.

PROVERBS 9:7-9 Be Wise and Accept Constructive Counsel

Proverbs 9:7-9 Updated American Standard Version (UASV)

7 He who corrects a scoffer gets himself abuse,
 and he who reproves a wicked man gets injury.[19]
8 Do not reprove a scoffer, or he will hate you;
 reprove a wise man, and he will love you.
9 Give instruction to a wise man, and he will be still wiser;
 teach[20] a righteous man, and he will increase in learning.

He who corrects a scoffer gets himself abuse: The verb translated **correct** (Heb. *yasar*) means to offer corrective counsel with the intention of improving the behavior of another. As discipline it need not come across as punishment, it is simply straight talk, withholding no punches, being very direct in teaching ones how to live their lives in the reverential fear of God so that they become wise from the life lessons before they are tempted by this wicked world and those alienated from God that would put them to the test.

The Hebrew word rendered **scoffer** (*lets*) is referring to someone who jeers, mocks, ridicules or treats someone with contempt. The person ridiculing another builds up resentment, anger, and hatred for the one trying to help make his path straight. Here the scoffer or ridiculer is one who resists being offered constructive correction and instruction. The **abuse** (Heb. *qalon*) is what one receives

---

[19] Lit *a blemish*
[20] Lit *make known to*

for his efforts at trying to give direction to a scoffer, which is utter contempt, disrespect, and dishonor.

And he who reproves a wicked man gets injury: This line is quite similar to the first line in meaning. **Reprove** (Heb. *yakach*) is similar in meaning to correct and has the same strong sense offering another straight talk, withholding no punches, being very direct in teaching ones how to live their life. The slight difference here with *yakach* **reprove** over *yasar* **correct** is that *yakach* carries a value judgment, implying that the one being reproved is guilty. When we look at the Hebrew word for wicked (*rasha*), we get the same implication of guilt, as the evil person is unrighteous, with a focus on the guilt of his being in violation of some standard.

Scoffers like to ridicule others, but if they are ridiculed themselves, they are unable to take it and will react badly, even violently. The wicked person has no appreciation for the one offering him reproof, to help him on the path of life. It can be very unwise to try and teach the beneficial truths of God's Word to someone who has utter contempt for you and the truth you are trying to share, for he will only ridicule your efforts. In your endeavor to reach the honest hearted with the good news of the kingdom, you need to be careful not to get too involved in debates and extensive argumentation with ridiculers.

Do not reprove a scoffer, or he will hate you: **Reprove** renders the same word that was used in 9:7b. **Scoffer** is as was used in 9:7a. **Scoffers** and **hate** are used in Proverbs 1:22, where the question is asked, "How long, O simple ones, will you love being simple-minded? And how long will scoffers delight in their scoffing and fools **hate knowledge**?"

Reprove a wise man, and he will love you: This line is the beginning of three lines (9:8b-9) that will contrast the first three lines of 9:7-8a. **Reprove** renders the same word from the previous line and that was used in 9:7b.

Truly **wise** (Heb. *chakam*) **ones** can talk frankly to each other with straight talk, holding nothing back and help each other to improve or to correct themselves where needed. The wise has a capacity for insight, understanding, and discernment. Here **love you** has the sense of respecting you.

Give instruction to a wise man, and he will be still wiser: Why will a wise person love or respect you for giving him reproof? Because he knows that through correction "he will be still wiser."

Teach a righteous man, and he will increase in learning: Increase in learning is one who continues to take in knowledge. No one is too wise or too old to keep learning.

If we are to be taught by wisdom, there will be times when we must accept correction and reproof. Of course, most of us tend to bristle at such times, yet it becomes easier as we mature in the faith. A scoffer is a ridiculer, one who expresses derision or scorn about somebody or something. This one does not receive correction well at all and has a dislike of anyone so offering. The wicked are in a whole other category, as they are blinded by their hatred for others, especially anyone suggesting they need help.

Therefore, it is a waste of time to attempt to offer 'what is holy [Scriptural wisdom] to dogs or throw your pearls [Scriptural wisdom] in front of pigs, lest they trample them with their feet, and turn around and tear you to pieces.' (Matt. 7:6) These ones will only ridicule any attempt that we make at sharing the good news with them. We can look to the apostle Paul, who while teaching some Jews in Antioch, came across some, who just wanted to do nothing but contradict him. What was Paul's response? He told them "since you thrust [Scripture] aside and judge yourselves unworthy of eternal life, behold, we are turning to the Gentiles." Acts 13:45-46

There will come times when we are trying to share the good news, and they will look to just debate, criticize, and argue with us. If it is they alone, it would be best just to walk away, letting it be their loss. However, if it is a public place of some sort, and others are listening intently at how you answer the challenges, it may be best to offer a reasonable answer, then express that you are not here to argue, and walk away. If you had not offered the parting answer, the others may have thought you did not have an answer.

The Christian is to be different from the world of humankind that surrounds them. As a disciple of Christ, we need to cultivate a love for discipline. The Word of God corrects us every time we pick it up. Yes, it is difficult to hear where we are falling short, but we should never be offended by correction, even if it is coming from a human representative of God. For some who have years on them, they may believe that with gray hair, they are wise from life experience. Even so, the Bible is filled with knowledge, understanding, and wisdom, from God, who has no beginning, and we will never live long enough, that we do not need counsel from time to time.

PROVERBS 4:23 Safeguard Your Heart

Proverbs 4:23 Updated American Standard Version (UASV)

23 Keep your heart with all vigilance,
  for from it flow the springs of life.

Keep your heart with all vigilance: The **heart** (Heb. *lēḇ*) in the Old Testament seldom has anything to do specifically with emotions. The heart is the "center of the physical, mental, and spiritual life of humans. The heart and the intellect are closely connected, the heart being the seat of intelligence."[21] The **heart** is to be **kept** (Heb. *nā·ṣǎr*) with all **vigilance** (Heb. *miš·mār*). To **keep** has the sense of safety: to keep, protect, or preserve something safe from injury, harm, or danger. It suggests a relationship with the protector. (Psa. 40:12) **Vigilance** means *to guard* or *keep careful watch over* for protection against possible danger or difficulties. It is constant reminders that keep these things close to the heart. This is why the writers of the Hebrew Old Testament repeated things so often or made the same point but in different ways. Without constant watchfulness, the heart can be caught off guard and lured into wrongdoing. If you keep a careful watch over your mind and your eyes, you will, in essence, be keeping a careful watch over your heart.

For from it flow the springs of life: From it, namely, the heart, figuratively, the mind, the element of a person that enables them to be aware of the world and their

---

[21] Gerald P. Cowen, "Heart", in Holman Illustrated Bible Dictionary, ed. Chad Brand, Charles Draper, Archie England et al., 731 (Nashville, TN: Holman Bible Publishers, 2003).

experiences, to think, and to feel; the faculty of consciousness and thought. The centerpiece of it all is the mind. Our moods, behaviors and body responses result from the way we view things. It is a proven fact that we cannot experience any event in any way, shape, or form unless we have processed it with our mind first. No event can depress us; it is our perception of that event that will depress us. If we are only sad over an event, our thoughts will be rational, but if we are depressed wrathful, or anxious about an event, our thinking will be bent and irrational, distorted and utterly wrong.

It may be difficult for each of us to wrap our mind around it, but we are superb at telling ourselves outright lies and half-truths, repeatedly throughout each day. In fact, some of us are so good at it that it has become our reality and led to annoyance, stress, irritation, anger, even depression, and anxiety. In many ways, our lives are somehow defined by the thoughts stored in and running through the heart or mind. How we think is how we feel.

PROVERBS 27:11 We Can Find Real Purpose In Life

Proverbs 27:11 Updated American Standard Version (UASV)

¹¹ Be wise, my son, and make my heart glad,
   that I may return a word to my reproacher.[22]

It is very clear from God's Word, we can find real purpose in life by worshipping the true God. His Word encourages us to give him the praise, honor, and obedience that he deserves. (Eccl. 12:13; Rev. 4:11) When we live our life in this way, we achieve something that is astonishing to consider: We literally have an effect on our Creator in a positive way. Indeed, he urges us: "Be wise . . . and make my heart glad." (Prov. 27:11) Stop and ponder this for just a moment, when we make wise decisions based on the principles found in God's Word, something that we were actually designed to do, we bring joy to the heart of our heavenly Father.

Why? Two reasons really: **First**, because God cares for us deeply and wants us to reap the benefits of his design, his guidance. (Isa. 48:17-18) **Second**, because Satan, in front of the angels called God a liar, further saying that God was withholding good from man and that man was selfish and would reject God when he realized he could walk alone. When we freely choose God over our fallen flesh and see the benefits, God is vindicated from the false accusations of the Devil. The Greek word (*diabolos*) rendered Devil means "slanderer." Really, there is no greater purpose in life than our worshipping the Sovereign of all creation and living in such a way that it brings joy to his heart.

---

[22] I.e. *that I may reply to him who reproaches me*

Be wise, my son, and make my heart glad: The idea of a son causing his father to rejoice is found throughout the book of Proverbs. The Hebrew (*chakam*) rendered **be wise** here is referring to a father urging his son to exercise good judgment, to have a special kind of understanding. **Be wise** is a command in the masculine to acquire and exercise good judgment and understanding, showing himself to be wise, which is here addressed to the **son**. **Make my heat glad** means make me happy or make me rejoice.

that I may return a word to my reproacher: Namely, 'that I [God] may reply or **answer** (Heb. *dabar*) to him who reproaches me.' Not that God literally needs to justify himself or personally respond to Satan's false accusations, his criticisms. Rather, it is us who offers that reply every time we choose God over our fallen flesh. The Hebrew word (*charaph*) rendered **reproach** is referring to Satan's criticism toward God. Satan the Devil has **treated God with contempt**, insulting him, reproaching him, taunting him, ridiculing him, defying him, i.e., speaking false words that besmirched and temporarily harmed God's good name among God's creation. Satan has spoken evil of God, he had mocked his sovereignty.

The False Accusations of Satan

(1) Satan called God a liar and said he was not to be trusted, as to the life or death issue.

(2) Satan's challenge, therefore, took into question the right and legitimacy of God's rightful place as the Universal Sovereign.

(3) Satan also suggested that people would remain obedient to God only as long as their submitting to God was to their benefit.

(4) Satan all but said that humankind was able to walk on his own, there being no need for dependence on God.

(5) Satan argued that man could be like God, choosing for himself what is right and wrong.

(6) Satan claimed that God's way of ruling was not in the best interests of humans, and they could do better without God.

God Settles the Issues

There is one thing that Satan did not challenge, namely, the power of God. Satan did not suggest that God was unable to destroy him as an opposer. However, he did challenge God's way of ruling, not His right to rule. Therefore, a moral issue must be settled.

An illustration of how God chose to deal with the issue can be demonstrated in human terms. A neighbor down the street slandered a man, who had a son and daughter. The slanderer said that he was not a good father, i.e., he withheld good from his children and was so overbearing, to the point of being abusive. The slanderer stated that the children would be better off without their father. He further argued that the children had no real love for their father and only obeyed him because of the food and shelter. How should the father deal with these false, i.e., slanderous accusations? If he were to go down the road and pummel the slanderer, it would only validate the lies, making the neighbors believe the accuser is telling the truth.

The answer lies with his family as they can serve as his witnesses. (Pro 27:11; Isa 43:10) If the children stay obedient and grow to be successful adults, turning out to be loving, caring, honest people with spotless character, it proves the accusations false. If the children accept the lies and rebel and grow up to be despicable people, it just further validates that they would have been better off by staying with the father. This is how God chose to deal with the issues. The issues that were raised must be settled beyond all reasonable doubt.

If God had destroyed the rebellious three: Satan, Adam, and Eve; he would not have resolved the issues of

(1) Whether man could walk on his own,

(2) if he would be better off without his Creator,

(3) if God's rulership were not best, and

(4) if God were hiding good from man.

(5) In addition, there was an audience of untold billions of angelic spirit creatures looking on.

If God destroyed without settling things, these spirit persons would be following God out of dreadful fear, not love, fear of displeasing God. Moreover, say He did kill them and start over, and ten thousand years down the road (with billions of humans now on earth), the issues were raised again, He would have to destroy billions of people again, and again, and again all throughout time, until these issues were laid to rest.

What God has done is, allow time to pass, and the issues to be resolved. Man thought he was better off without God and could walk on his own. In addition, man has attempted every kind of rulership imaginable, and one must ask, 'have they proven themselves better than rulership under the sovereignty of their Creator?' (Proverbs 1:30-33; Isaiah 59:4, 8) Sadly, the issues must be taken up to the brink of destroying man. (Rev 11:18) Otherwise, the argument would be that if given enough time, they could have turned things around. If man goes up to the point of destroying himself and Armageddon comes at the last minute, it will have set a case law, solved the issue, and the Bible can serve as the example forever. If the issues of God's sovereignty or the loyalty of His created creatures, angelic or human, is ever questioned again, we would have the Holy Bible that will serve as a law established based on previous verdicts of not guilty, please see below.

What Have the Results Been?

(1) God does not cause evil and suffering. Romans 9:14.

(2) The fact that God has allowed evil, pain, and suffering have shown that independence from God has not brought about a better world. Jeremiah 8:5, 6, 9.

(3) God's permission of evil, pain, and suffering has also proved that Satan has not been able to turn all humans away from God. Exodus 9:16; 1 Samuel 12:22; Hebrews 12:1.

(4) The fact that God has permitted evil, pain, and suffering to continue has provided proof that only God, the Creator, has the capability and the right to rule over humankind for their eternal blessing and happiness. Ecclesiastes 8:9.

(5) Satan has been the god of this world since the sin in Eden (over 6,000 years), and how has that worked out for man, and what has been the result of man's course of independence from God and his rule? Matthew 4:8-9; John 16:11; 2 Corinthians 4:3-4; 1 John 5:19; Psalm 127:1.

Satan's impact on the earth's activities has carried with it conflict, evil and death, and his rulership has been by means of deception, power and his own self-interest. He has demonstrated himself an unfit ruler of everything. Therefore, God is now completely vindicated in putting an end to this corrupted rebel along with all who have shared in his evil deeds.—Romans 16:20.

God has tolerated evil, sickness, pain, suffering, and death until our day in order to resolve all the issues raised by Satan. We are self-centered in thinking that this has only pained us. Imagine that you are holding a rope on a sinking ship that 20 other men, women, and children are clinging to when your child loses her grip and falls into the ocean. You can hold the rope, saving 20 people, or you can let go and attempt to rescue your daughter. God has been watching the suffering of billions from the day of Adam and Eve's sin. Moreover, it has been His great love for us, which causes Him to cling to the rope of issues, saving us from a future of repeated issues. Nevertheless, he will not allow this evil to remain forever. He has set a fixed time when He will end this wicked system of Satan's rule.

Daniel 11:27 Updated American Standard Version (UASV)

[27] As for both kings, their heart will be inclined to do what is evil, and they will speak lies to each other at the same table; but it will not succeed, for the end is still to come <u>at the appointed time</u>.

Unlike what many people of the world may think (the world that lies in the hands of Satan), being obedient to God is not difficult. We simply must set our pride aside and accept that the wisdom of God is so far greater than our own and accept that He has worked for the good of obedient humankind, as He loves each one of us.

Matthew 7:21 Updated American Standard Version (UASV)

[21] "Not everyone who says to me, 'Lord, Lord,' will enter the kingdom of heaven, but <u>the one who does the will of my Father</u> who is in heaven.

1 John 2:15-17 Updated American Standard Version (UASV)

[15] Do not love the world or the things in the world. If anyone loves the world, the love of the Father is not in him. [16] For all that is in the world, the lust of the flesh and the lust of the eyes and the boastful pride of life, is not from the Father, but is from the world. [17] The world is passing away, and its lusts; but the one who does the will of God remains forever.

As Christians, there is a love we must not have. We must 'not love the world or anything in it.' Instead, we need to keep from becoming infected by the corruption of unrighteous human society that is alienated from God and must not breathe in its mental disposition or be moved by its sinful dominant attitude. (Ephesians 2:1, 2; James 1:27) If we were to have the views of those in the world that are in opposition to God, "the love of the Father" would not be in us. — James 4:4.

PROVERBS 8:13 Turn Away from Morally Objectionable Behavior

Proverbs 8:13 Updated American Standard Version (UASV)

¹³ The fear of Jehovah is hatred of evil.
Pride and arrogance and the way of evil
   and the perverted mouth I hate.

The fear of Jehovah is hatred of evil: Again, the **fear of Jehovah** is mentioned, meaning that we possess a reverential awe of our Creator, hating what he hates. "Fear of [Jehovah] Wisdom does not stand alone. It is closely connected with fearing God and involves a proper attitude of respect and obedience."[23] The Hebrew word (*sane*) rendered **hatred** appears about 145 times in the Bible and can range from a weak **dislike**, shun, not love, a lacking love, and compassion, to an intense hatred. Here in this context (*sane*) **hatred** is to abhor, detest, loathe, to dislike intensely, to feel hostility or an aversion towards evil. **Evil** (Heb. *ra*) is anything that is morally objectionable behavior based on the moral standards found in God's Word. Those practicing what is evil, not morally pure, sever their relationship with God.

Pride and arrogance and the way of evil: The Hebrew noun (*geah*) rendered **pride** is the quality of one who has an attitude of superiority, believing that he is superior to others. The one has an unreasonable and unwarranted or undue and an excessive self-esteem of himself. He is haughty and arrogant. The Hebrew noun (*gaon*) rendered **arrogance** has a very similar meaning. He is full of himself,

---

[23] John D. Barry, Michael R. Grigoni, Michael S. Heiser et al., Faithlife Study Bible (Bellingham, WA: Logos Bible Software, 2012), Pr 8:13.

having or revealing an exaggerated sense of his own importance or abilities. He is conceited, that is, he has an unwarranted and undue high status of himself, which is a moral failure on his part. **The way of evil** means one's wicked ways, his following evil paths that lead to bad or wicked behavior or conduct.

And the perverted mouth I hate: The Hebrew noun (*tahpukot*) that is rendered **perverted** is one who willfully deviates from what is good and in this case with his **mouth** (*peh*), that is, speech, what he says. In the Scriptures perversity usually applies to one's words, what is said that is morally crooked (distorted, dishonest, unscrupulous, unprincipled, untrustworthy, corrupt) from the moral standard set out in the Word of God.

Pride, arrogance, immoral behavior, and mouth of perversity should be no part of a Christian life. If we hate what is evil, it will protect us against the deceptive desires of this world. Therefore, it is paramount that we all seek wisdom. Those who live irresponsible lives, regardless of their intelligence, are stupid ones. Really, these ones lack wisdom. Wisdom gives its owner the right path to life and strength to deal with adversities. Choices that are made by ones who lack prudence and discretion are more than likely end badly.

PROVERBS 19:20 Become Wiser Throughout Your Life Until You Are Wise

Proverbs 19:20 Updated American Standard Version (UASV)

20 Listen to counsel and accept instruction,
   that you may gain wisdom in your end.[24]

The Bible helps us to avoid foolish decisions. Certainly, every one of us needs such help for we all are imperfect and fall short many times. No doubt, since we have accepted Christ, we have made changes in our lives to bring ourselves into line with what we have learned from the Bible.

Listen to counsel and accept instruction: The Hebrew term (*shama*) rendered **listening** means to listen, to hear, to pay close attention, and respond, heed, or obey on the basis of having heard. (Prov. 5:12) If we are listening and **accepting** (Heb. *qabal*), it means that we are truly *heeding* and *paying attention* to the wise counsel. **Instruction** (Heb. *musar*) hear means that we are accepting, heeding, paying attention to, applying the teaching of the principles of God's Word for life. We are training ourselves to improve ourselves, to gain control over ourselves.

that you may gain wisdom in your end: The whole purpose of line 1 is so that we may gain wisdom. **Wisdom** (Heb. *chokmah*) is sound judgment, based on knowledge and understanding. It is the balanced application of that knowledge to answer difficulties, achieve objectives, sidestep or ward off dangers, not to mention helping others to accomplish the same. The wise person is often

---

[24] I.e. *in your future*

contrasted with the foolishness or stupid person. (Deut. 32:6; Prov. 11:29; Eccles. 6:8) **The end** (Heb. *acharith*) can mean that if we are accepting, heeding, paying attention to, applying the teaching of the principles of God's Word for life; training ourselves to improve ourselves, to gain control over ourselves, in the closing days of our life, we will have become wise. However, more often in Proverbs, the Hebrew term *acharith* means the result **when** we have listened to counsel and accepted instruction.

Yes, the gaining of wisdom is accumulative over time. We do not have to take in wise counsel throughout our lives to finally be wise when we are eighty years old. As we grow in knowledge and understanding because we have truly *heeded* and *paid attention* to the wise counsel found in God's Word, we are truly *becoming* **wiser** in each of those moments in our lives. How fast we become wiser is dependent on how we react to the counsel of God's Word. First and foremost, we must make certain that we have a correct understanding of what the Bible author meant by the words that he used. Second, if the counsel is not palatable to our way of thinking due to imperfect human nature, we set aside what we feel, think, and believe and sincerely express appreciation for the counsel and work at applying it in our lives. In **the end**, we will find the outcome of our doing so will make us wiser and wiser until we have become wise.

PROVERBS 3:13 Happy Is the One Who Finds Wisdom

Proverbs 3:13 Updated American Standard Version (UASV)

¹³ Happy is a man who finds wisdom,
  and the one who gains understanding,

Many Christians might not be aware of these "beatitudes," as well as others in the Book of Proverbs (8:32, 34; 14:21; 16:20; 20:7; 28:14; 29:18). The RSV, LEB, CSB, and the UASV render the Hebrew word (*asre*) "happy, while the ESV and the NASB render it "blessed." **Happy, blessed**: (Heb. *asre*; Gr. *makarios*) *Asre* occurs 11 times in the Hebrew Old Testament and *makarios* 50 times in the Greek New Testament. Happiness and being highly favored by God characterize this joy. It is speaking of a person who is content, full of joy. This is not to be confused with the Hebrew word *barak* which means, "to bless," as in a divine blessing. The Hebrew barak and the Greek *eulogeo* is the act of being blessed, while the Hebrew *asre* and Greek *makarios* is the state or condition of the person who is being blessed, who is a highly favored one. – 1 Ki 10:8; Ps 1:1; 119:1-2; Pro. 14;21; 16:20; Matt. 5:3-11; 11:6; 13:16; Lu 1:45; John 13:17; 20:29; Ac 20:35; Rom. 4:7-8 to mention just a few.

As we know by now, wisdom is personified in the book of Proverbs as a female, which helps the reader to better understand the different qualities that make up wisdom.[25] Wisdom is the ability to apply knowledge

---

[25] Wisdom is mentioned in the book of Proverbs 46 times!

correctly. One may have substantial knowledge but lacks the ability to use it because wisdom is absent.

Understanding is the ability to see how the facets, characteristics, features, or parts of something have a significant connection with or bearing to one another, to be able to picture the whole matter and not just remote pieces of information. Proverbs 9:10 (NASB) says, "Knowledge of the Holy One is understanding." This means that if we are ever to have a deeper understanding of things, it must be in conjunction with Jehovah God and his will and purposes. If we possess understanding, we are the type of person that can connect the new information with what we already know, which means, "knowledge is easy to one who has understanding." (Pro. 14:6, NASB) Verse 13 is reminiscent of this repeated language found in the book of Proverbs where a young man "who finds a wife," which "is a good thing," as "her worth is far above jewels." (Pro. 18:22; 31:10) Yes, finding wisdom is like finding a worthy wife.

PROVERBS 8:10-11 Wisdom Is More Precious Than All Else

Proverbs 8:10-11 Updated American Standard Version (UASV)

[10] Take my instruction instead of silver,
　　and knowledge rather than choice gold,
[11] for wisdom is better than jewels,
　　and all that you may desire cannot compare with her.

Take my instruction instead of silver: Here the Hebrew verb **take** (*laqach*) expresses a command that has the sense of grasping or taking hold of, namely, willingly accepting, receiving, or choosing what is offered. Thus, we are to grasp or take hold of, willingly choose wisdom's instruction. **My instruction** is the instruction coming from wisdom. **Instructions**: (Heb. *piqqudim*) This Hebrew noun means instructions, precepts, directions, procedures, regulation, i.e., a principle or rule concerning the personal conduct that is to be obeyed within a community.

And knowledge rather than choice gold: Knowledge (Heb. *daath*) is possession of information learned by personal experience, observation, or study. The Bible strongly urges us to seek and treasure accurate knowledge, as it is far superior to choice gold, which is gold of the highest purity.

For wisdom is better than jewels: The conjunction **for** is introducing the reasons as to why we should take wisdom's instruction and knowledge. The adjective **better** is of a greater value. **Wisdom:** (Heb. *chokmah*) is sound judgment, based on knowledge and understanding. It is the balanced application of that knowledge to answer difficulties, achieve objectives, sidestep or ward off dangers, not to mention helping others to accomplish the same. The wise person is often contrasted with the foolishness or stupid person.

And all that you may desire cannot compare with her: Here **all that you may desire** means all of the things that you may desire.

Correctly, the truth is that wisdom is far more valuable than silver or choice gold. World events have demonstrated repeatedly, at any given time, the economy can crash, and money becomes worthless, with survival being found in the choices of the wise one. Wisdom's teachings are priceless, because they lead to life everlasting, something no amount of money can buy, as it is an undeserved gift from God. Even now, wisdom can deliver true happiness and offer protection to the one who is wise.

PROVERBS 9:10 We Cannot Have Wisdom Without Knowledge

Proverbs 9:10 Updated American Standard Version (UASV)

10 The fear of Jehovah is the beginning of wisdom,
  and the knowledge of the Holy One is understanding.

The fear of Jehovah is the beginning of wisdom: "The fear of Jehovah" is the repeated theme of wisdom found in the book of Proverbs.[26] One who fears Jehovah, he has the qualities of humility (15:33; 22:4), wisdom (1:7), possessing faithfulness and Godly love (16:6), and a concern for his relationship with God (2:5; 9:10). In the book of Proverbs, fear of Jehovah is related to faith in God that is constantly seeking understanding.[27] In what way is "the fear of Jehovah" "the beginning of knowledge" and 'the beginning of wisdom'? (9:10) If we did not have a fear of Jehovah (i.e., **not a** morbid dread of him but rather a profound reverence and awe in the presence of such an all-powerful person), we would have no knowledge, for the Father is the Creator of all things and the Author of the Spirit-inspired Scriptures.

And the knowledge of the Holy One is understanding: Knowledge (Heb. *daath*) is possession of information learned by personal experience, observation, or study. The Bible strongly urges us to seek and treasure accurate knowledge, as it is far superior to gold. Here Holy One has a plural ending, which is used at times to refer saintly persons, heavenly beings, or angels (see Psa. 34:9;

---

[26] (cf. 1:29; 2:5; 9:10; 10:27; 14:26, 27; 15:16, 33; 16:6; 19:23; 22:4; 23:17)

[27] Leo G. Perdue, *Wisdom & Creation: The Theology of Wisdom Literature* (Nashville: Abingdon, 1994), p. 79.

Job 5:1; 15:15; Zech. 14:5), so this has caused some to see the plural here referring to "holy men." However, the parallelism here evidences otherwise, the pluralism is used to emphasize the holiness of God. Another example of this is the plural form of God (elim; elohim), is used when referring to other gods, such as at Exodus 15:11 ("gods"). It is also used as the plural of majesty, dignity, and excellence. There is no wisdom apart from God. **Understanding** (Heb. *bunah*) is the ability to see how the parts or aspects of something are connected to one another. One who possesses understanding can see the big picture (the entire matter) and not just the isolated facts. A true **understanding** of all facets of human life involves our appreciation of its relation to God and his will and purposes

We cannot have wisdom without knowledge. Furthermore, if we lack the fear of Jehovah, we will not use whatever knowledge we acquire to honor the Creator. What is the crucial criterion for wisdom? It is the fear of Jehovah. Of course, this is not some morbid dread but is a reverential awe for Jehovah God. We may be very studious and have acquired a storehouse of Bible knowledge. However, if it has not gotten down into our heart, the seat of motivation, moving us into reverential awe of Jehovah, we will not have the wisdom to apply the knowledge in a right way. Moreover, the knowledge of Jehovah is crucial if we are to gain insight or understanding, a facet of wisdom.

PROVERBS 6:25-26 Do Not Desire the Immoral Woman's Beauty

Proverbs 6:25-26 Updated American Standard Version (UASV)

²⁵ Do not desire her beauty in your heart,
    and do not let her capture you with her eyelashes;[28]
²⁶ for because of a prostitute, a man is reduced to a loaf of bread,
    but a wife of another man hunts down a precious soul.[29]

²⁶ [Although the price of a prostitute may be as much as a loaf of bread,
    another man's wife hunts the precious life].[30]

Do not desire her beauty in your heart: Here (Heb. $ḥā·mǎḏ$) **desire** is being used in the bad sense in that the young man is being warned against strongly wanting, lusting after, coveting the beauty of another man's wife.

And do not let her capture you with her eyelashes: Here (Heb. $lā·qǎḥ$) **capture** is referring to the young man being seduced or being led astray by the alluring eyes of another man's wife. The Hebrew ($ǎp̄·ʿǎp·pǎ·yim$) is rendered **eyelashes** here but is literally "eyelids," which is referring to how a woman uses her alluring eyes to attract the attention of men.

---

[28] I.e. alluring eyes
[29] I.e. life
[30] Duane A. Garrett, vol. 14, Proverbs, Ecclesiastes, Song of Songs, The New American Commentary, 100 (Nashville: Broadman & Holman Publishers, 1993).

For because of a prostitute, a man is reduced to a loaf of bread: A prostitute is a person, in particular, a woman, who engages in sexual activity for payment. It seems that Solomon is saying that an adulterous wife being referred to as a prostitute may cost as much as a loaf of bread.

But a wife of another man hunts down a precious soul: The adulteress wife endangers the "precious soul," or life, of her adulterous partner. The Hebrew (ṣûḏ) **hunts down** is referring to the husband of the adulteress doing after the adulterous young man, who had sexual relations with his wife, intending to cause him bodily harm or kill him.

Exodus 20:14, "You shall not commit adultery," which means that we need to value the sanctity of marriage, to remain faithful at times of temptation. At Matthew 5:28 Jesus states, "But I say to you that everyone who looks at a woman with lustful intent has already committed adultery with her in his heart." (ESV) Jesus identified the preliminaries, which was a sin in and of itself, that lead up to the sinful act of adultery, as "lustful intent." Focus on the word "intent." This is not a man walking along who catches sight of a beautiful woman and has an indecent thought, which he then dismisses (that is not lusting). It is not even a man in the same situation that has an indecent thought, who goes on to entertain and cultivate that thought (this is lusting and is a sin). No, this is a man that is staring, gazing at a woman with the intent of lusting, and is looking at the woman, with the intention of peaking her interest and desire, to get her to lust.

Verse 25 of chapter 26 in Proverbs warns the son against just that, do not get "lustful intent" in your heart because of her beauty. Yes, even when the evil woman is seeking to flame such desires. Aside from the fact that it violates God's Law, for mere moments of immediate gratification at a very inexpensive price, you are risking your life on a wife, who has a husband that will take your precious life.

James 1:14-15 Updated American Standard Version (UASV)

¹⁴ But each one is tempted when he is carried away and enticed by his own desire.[31] ¹⁵ Then the desire when it has conceived gives birth to sin, and sin when it is fully grown brings forth death.

> James states **but each one is tempted**, which signifies that temptation is on an individual basis. The temptation is not another individual's problem but is an individual choice that one gives into or rejects. James also writes one is tempted when he is **carried away and enticed by his desire**, which exposes that the problem of temptation lies not with God, but rather it is in oneself. James says that temptation is always directed at the desire of one's heart. Therefore, God is not the one who is causing the temptation, but the temptation comes through the enticement of one's lust within his heart.
>
> The Greek word James uses here for **enticed** is *deleazo*, which means to "*lure as bait.*" (Vine 1996, 203) James tells us in the passage that the underlying motivation for all temptation is selfish desire, that all temptations spring from man's **desire** to satisfy his own flesh and personal forbidden desires. This means the temptation that Satan offers to people always deals with that which is pleasurable to man and appeals to his desires. This is not to say that human desires in and of itself are wrong. Moreover, human pleasure is not bad in and of itself. Satan has corrupted the desires of the flesh, which was perfectly natural before the sin of Adam. For example, there was a natural desire for a physical relationship between man and woman. After

---

[31] Or "own *lust*"

the fall, Paul tells us that it has become a standard practice "For their women [to] exchange natural relations for those that are contrary to nature," i.e., homosexuality. (Rom. 1:26) Once the lust is manifested in the heart then the more it lingers there without being dealt with then it will begin to carry away the individual with the enticement of what that fulfilled lust can bring.

Temptation always begins with an enticement towards one's lust or an unwarranted desire. If not cast down, one then is carried away by the bait of the enticement. Then soon after, one will take the bait, give in to the temptation, and satisfy the lust of his flesh. It is for this reason that James writes **then the desire when it has conceived gives birth to sin**. James continues with the progression stating **sin when it is fully-grown brings forth death**. Once the desire is conceived, or once the individual gives acts upon that temptation by giving into its evil desire, it gives birth to sin that can lead to death.

James is telling these believers that once sin is conceived and begins to take root in the heart if it is not dealt with, it will become full grown within the heart, to attain what their hearts desire. James makes it very clear that once we give in to the temptation of that lust, it will inevitably give birth to sin. What was meant to produce pleasure and satisfaction, now only causes chaos and devastation. James warns these believers that the only result of fulfilling their lust brought about death. This death could for some have led to physical death depending upon the lust they were giving into. James has a deeper meaning in the fact that it was causing spiritual death to these believers when they gave into sin.

Again, we can see from Adam and Eve that when they ate of the fruit, they did so out of their desire and pleasure for power and control that stemmed from their lust. When they ate of the fruit, the promise of fulfillment only resulted in death. When Adam and Eve ate of the fruit, they faced spiritual death, in the fact that their sin had separated them from God. In turn, because of the curse, they would also suffer physical death due to their sin. James is warning these believers of the serious danger of temptation and the consequences if they were to give in to their lust. James wants his readers to understand that for the one who persisted in his temptation and living in that manner, and then, in the end, he would face eternal destruction. Paul wrote in Romans 7:20-21, "For when you were slaves of sin, you were free in regard to righteousness. Therefore what benefit were you then deriving from the things of which you are now ashamed? For the outcome of those things is death."[32]

---

[32] Thomas D. Lea, *THE BOOK OF JAMES*, vol. 17, CPH New Testament Commentary (Cambridge, OH: Christian Publishing House, 2017), 28-29.

PROVERBS 12:1 Discipline is Absolutely Necessary

Proverbs 12:1 Updated American Standard Version (UASV)

12 He who loves discipline loves knowledge,
  but he who hates reproof is stupid.

He who loves discipline loves knowledge: We have a masculine singular verb (*ōhēb*) translated **he who loves**, which means *whoever loves*. The one loving **discipline, correction,** and reproof loves **knowledge**, which leads to a successful life.

Discipline (Heb. *musar*) is repeatedly mentioned throughout the book of Proverbs. In the Scriptures, discipline often carries the sense of correction, admonition, rebuke, or chastisement. It is the practice or methods of teaching and enforcing acceptable patterns of behavior: correction, admonition, or modification, whether it is self-discipline or the discipline of another. According to *The Expositor's Bible Commentary*, it "denotes the training of the moral nature, involving the correcting of waywardness toward folly." (Garland and Longman 2008, 48) Do we need this training? Whether we are disciplining ourselves, or are being disciplined by another, by grasping the counsel within the Scriptures, and then applying it in our lives, it moves us to become a better servant of God. If we are to move over from inherited death to life, we need discipline. **Knowledge** (Heb. *daath*) is possession of information learned by personal experience, observation, or study. It includes wisdom, understanding, insight, and the ability to live successfully apply what has been taken into one's heart and mind. The Bible strongly urges us to seek and treasure accurate knowledge, as it is far superior to gold. – Prov. 8:10; 20:15.

but he who hates reproof is stupid: The Hebrew (*sane*) rendered **hate** means to abhor, detest, loathe, to dislike intensely, to feel apathy for or hostility for someone or something. **Reproof:** (Heb. *tokachath*) has the sense of an act or expression of criticism or disapproval, even condemnation. It is speaking strong words of disapproval, which may also include punishment. (Prov. 1:23, 25, 30; 3:11; 5:12; 6:23; 10:17; 12:1; 13:18; 15:5, 10, 31, 32; 27:5; 29:1, 15) The Hebrew term (*baar*) rendered **stupid**, which is only used in the wisdom literature within the Old Testament. In Psalm 73:22, *baar* means *beastlike* or *brutish*. It is what is used to describe foolish ones, those who have no sense.

In our human imperfection, there is a tendency to hate or resent reproof (correction) and through the source that it is coming through, be it another human or the Word of God. If we give in to this hatred of reproof, it degrades us to be less than human, to being nothing more than a senseless unreasoning beast, who lacks moral discernment. Receptiveness to what is learned is a great form of self-discipline when we apply what is right and just, properly applying the information we receive.

If we are eager to improve our lives, we will crave discipline. He who is righteous is quick to apply the discipline he receives at home, from church leadership, from Christian friends, and especially God's Word. The words within the Scriptures are like ox goads that prod him to follow an upright path that leads to life. This one does not wait for knowledge to come his way, he seeks it out like hidden treasure, to make his course straight. Yes, one who loves discipline loves knowledge.

If we are going to find favor in the eyes of God, discipline is very much necessary, especially self-discipline. Discipline is correcting what is wrong or missing. Maybe we wish that we had a deeper knowledge of God's Word. Maybe we wish that we were more effective in sharing the

Word of God with others. (Matthew 24:14; 28:19-20; Ac 1:8) However, if we lack self-discipline, these things will never be a reality. This applies to every facet of our lives. For example, we live in a world that feeds the fallen flesh with immoral desires through every form of entertainment, and even simply going from one place to another, and especially the workplace. Is there not a need for self-discipline, in order to restrain the eye from focusing on improper sights? Moreover, Scripture tells us that all humans are mentally bent toward evil and our hearts are treacherous and unknowable. (Gen. 6:5; 8:21; Jer. 17:9) Therefore, immoral thinking can be cultivated in the recesses of the mind. Self-discipline is needed in order not to entertain, dwell or cultivate such thoughts.

The wicked one who hates reproof, on the other hand, he loves neither discipline or knowledge, so he remains brutish and beastlike in feeding his fallen flesh. Because he has given into his evil leanings, feeding his imperfect human tendencies, he has become less than human, an unreasoning animal, a brute, who lacks moral judgment. We must resolutely resist this leaning, this inclination.

PROVERBS 24:3-4 Knowledge, Wisdom and Understanding Brings Precious and Pleasant Qualities

Proverbs 24:3 Updated American Standard Version (UASV)

³ By wisdom a house is built,
   and by understanding it is established;

Wisdom does not just build up a house, a building, but rather a household, that is the family and its successful family life that makes up the house. (Compare Prov. 3:19-20; Ps 104:5-24.)

By wisdom a house is built: The Hebrew (בְּ- *bᵉ*) preposition here, **by**, is being used to *indicate* the means, wisdom, of how the house is built. Here **wisdom:** (Heb. *chokmah*) is using sound judgment, based on knowledge and understanding. It is the balanced application of that knowledge to answer difficulties, achieve objectives, sidestep or ward off dangers, not to mention helping others to accomplish the same. The wise person is often contrasted with the foolishness or stupid person. (Deut. 32:6; Prov. 11:29; Eccles. 6:8) Here its focus is on practical skills and management if the reference it to a literal building but if the reference is to the family within, it would also refer to a moral element. Here house (Heb. *banah*) could be taken literally as the physical building, or it could also be referring to the family within, the household.

and by understanding it is established: The Hebrew (-בְּ *bᵉ*) preposition here, **by**, is being used to *indicate* the means, understanding, of how it, the house, is established. **Understanding** (Heb. *bunah*) is the ability to see how the parts or aspects of something are connected to one another. One who possesses understanding can see the big picture (the entire matter) and not just the isolated facts. (Prov. 2:5; 9:10; 18:15.) Here the pronoun **it** is referring back to the **house** from line 1. Here establish (Heb. *kun*) corresponds to **built** from line 1. In other words, the **house**, practical skills, and management if the reference it to a literal building but if the reference is to the family within, it would also refer to a moral element, which is set up or founded upon understanding and by wisdom. It has the sense of *making secure*, *making firm*, or *making durable*.

How can wisdom build a house? If we are talking about a household, a family, **wisdom:** (Heb. *chokmah*) is using sound judgment, based on your knowledge and understanding. If the father and mother or even a single parent have the ability to make wise decisions based on their fully understanding their accurate knowledge of God's Word, life will be far easier, many difficulties can be avoided. Because the parents pass on this wisdom to their children, the family will grow spiritually.

Proverbs 24:4 Updated American Standard Version (UASV)

⁴ by knowledge the rooms are filled
with all precious and pleasant riches.

by knowledge the rooms are filled: The Hebrew (בְּ- *bᵉ*) preposition here, **by**, is being used to *indicate* the means, knowledge, of how the rooms are filled. **Knowledge** (Heb. *daath*) is possession of information learned by personal experience, observation, or study. It includes wisdom, understanding, insight, and the ability to live successfully apply what has been taken into one's heart and mind. The Bible strongly urges us to seek and treasure accurate knowledge, as it is far superior to gold. (Prov. 8:10; 20:15) Here rooms could be various rooms of a house if the house of verse 23 is literal. If this is the case, the next line is referring to literal furnishings and content.

with all precious and pleasant riches: The Hebrew word (*yaqar*) rendered **precious** is referring to the expensive cost of the content and furnishings of the rooms, which has the sense of *rare* and *splendid* in this context. The Hebrew word for **pleasant** (*naim*) pertains to or implies *acceptable* and *favorable*.

We need to realize that these **precious and pleasant riches** are not just material treasures but also include such qualities as true love, godly fear, and strong faith. If verse 23 is referring to a household, family, such qualities will certainly create a precious and pleasant family life. (Prov. 15:16-17; 1 Pet. 1:7) However, if we are to acquire these precious and pleasant qualities and others, we must bring the knowledge of God into our households, which will give us wisdom and understanding.

PROVERBS 10:8-9 The Wise of Heart or the One Foolish of Lips

Proverbs 10:8-9 Updated American Standard Version (UASV)

⁸ The wise of heart will heed commandments,
   but the one foolish of lips[33] will be trampled down.[34]

⁹ He who walks in integrity walks securely,
   but he who makes his paths crooked[35] will be known.[36]

The wise of heart will heed commandments: Back in 6:32, the author spoke of being in **want of heart**. This is one who is inexperienced, lacking good sense and wisdom, lacking good judgment or discernment. Here we have just the opposite person who is **wise of heart**. The heart (Heb. *leb*) is used figuratively as the location of a person's thoughts (mind), decisions, emotions, and knowledge of what is right from wrong. Thus, a person who is **wise of heart** is one who is sensible, possessing and showing good sense and good judgment in his decision making, as well as his thoughts and actions, which enable him to determine what is right and what is wrong.

The heart is very prominent in the Scriptures, as it is mentioned about a thousand times in one way or another. By far, the great majority of its occurrences in the Scriptures, the word "heart" (Heart, *leb*) is used *figuratively*. Servants of God cannot be **halfhearted** or **in want of heart**, or even **double hearted**. (Ps 12:2; Prov.

---

[33] I.e. the one speaking foolishly
[34] I.e. *will come to ruin*, or *will be destroyed*
[35] Or *perverts his ways*
[36] Or *will be found out*

10:13) As a reader of hearts, God can see any insincere or feigned behavior on our part. He is well aware of our actions and thinking, even when we are alone. He knows our heart condition, what we are trying to do with our lives. If our heart is good, and we love God's Word, he will know. (Josh. 1:8-9; Ps. 1:1-3; 119:97, 101, 105, and 165) A person who is **halfhearted** is lukewarmly worshiping God. (Ps 119:113; Rev. 3:16) This young man being tempted by adultery is **double hearted** (literally, with a heart and a heart), is trying to serve two masters (God and his flesh), or he is deceivingly saying one thing while thinking sinful thoughts to himself. (1 Ch. 12:33; Ps 12:2) Jesus clearly condemned such **double hearted** hypocrisy. – Matthew 15:7-8.

The wise one's **heeding** (Heb. *laqach*) of commandments means that he will be receptive to the commands, he will pay attention and obey the commands. He does this willingly. The Hebrew word (*mitsvah*) translated **commandments** was used in Proverbs 2:1; 3:1; and 4:4, where it was used in reference to the words and teachings of wisdom. **My words** refer to the Law (thoughts and ideas) that Solomon has embraced in an active faith and obedience, which he is teaching as well. The use of commandments here in this verse is referring simply to the good instruction, advice or counsel that one **receives**.

but the one foolish of lips will be trampled down: The expression foolish of lips is referring to the person who speaks foolishly or is a foolish talker. His senseless babbling will cause him to be trampled down. The Hebrew word for **fool** (*evil*) is referring to a simpleton, one who lacks good judgment. He lacks understanding and stubbornly so, who is both stupid in his actions and his words. The wise of heart is being contrasted with foolish of lips. Instead of being able to have the good judgment to recognize, let alone obey good instruction, advice or counsel that the foolish one **receives**, his senseless talk causes him to be **trampled down**, that is he will be brought to ruin. In other words, his foolish words that are spoken without thinking will bring him a lifetime of ruination, trouble, ending up with nothing.

He who walks in integrity walks securely: In the Bible, the expression "to walk" is figurative and illustrative and can mean to follow a certain course of action, as "Noah walked with God." (Gen. 6:9; 5:22) Those who walk with God follow the life course outlined by God's Word and will find his favor, that is, be pleasing to him. Pursuing such a life-course makes you different from most of the unbelievers. The Greek New Testament uses the same illustrative expression, contrasting two different courses of action sought by one before and after becoming a servant of God. (Eph. 2:2, 10; 4:17; 5:2) The Hebrew verb **walk** (*halak*) is expressing a life course that one will experience as a result of possessing the wisdom of God and the Hebrew noun **securely** (*betach*) is telling us that as compared to those ignoring or rejecting the wisdom of God, we will **walk ... securely**. This is not saying that we will absolutely be free from danger or injury but rather, Solomon is saying far more so than those who lack wisdom.

Hebrew terms relating to integrity have the root meaning of that which is "whole" or "complete." They often suggest moral soundness and uprightness. Those walking in **integrity** are unbending in devotion to Jehovah. For such blameless ones, he is a protective shield because they display true wisdom and conform to his righteous standards. This does not mean, though, that Jehovah will not allow you to be tested. He did so even with Job. "God is faithful," the apostle Paul noted to the Corinthians. In full he said, "No temptation has overtaken you but such as is common to man; and God is faithful, who will not allow you to be tempted beyond what you are able, but with the temptation will provide the way of escape also, so that you will be able to endure it." – 1 Corinthians 10:13.

**but he who makes his paths crooked will be known:
Paths crooked:** (Heb. *derākāy meaqqēsh*) means their ways are morally crooked, **perverse**, distorted, dishonest, and evasive when it is compared alongside the just, right and correct ways of the wise ones. The phrase "will be **known**" can be rendered will be "**found out.**" The one who perverts his ways (makes his paths crooked) will be found out (known). It is likely referring to being found out by other people as opposed to being found out by God because God would have already foreseen any perverted ways. God could never find out anything.

If you are always talking; there is no opportunity to learn anything. You acquire wisdom by listening to the good instruction, advice or counsel that you receive through others. Because you are sensible, possessing and showing good sense and good judgment in your decision making, you will then accept and obey these commands. However, the simpleton foolish one is only aware of his own ignorance because he is too busy babbling to learn anything. Therefore, he will eventually bring himself to ruin and anyone else in association with him. Therefore, if you may it a practice of walking down crooked paths (perverted ways), you will eventually be **found out** by others, who will likely never trust you when the time comes when you seriously want and need others to believe and trust you, but they will feel they cannot.

PROVERBS 12:24 The One Working Hard Succeeds

Proverbs 12:24 Updated American Standard Version (UASV)

24 The hand of the diligent will rule,
　while the slothful will be put to forced labor.

The hand of the diligent will rule: Hand (Heb. *yad*) is used figuratively and symbolically throughout the Scriptures. The hand here is used to represent the person himself, as a **diligent** (Heb. *charuts*) **hand** is a hardworking person. It is one who has or shows care and conscientiousness, concern in one's work or duties. The word Hebrew word (*mashal*) rendered **rule** means to exercise authority and power over others.

while the slothful will be put to forced labor: Here **slothful** (Heb. *remiyyah*) means to be *lazy* or *sluggish*. The sense of the Hebrew *remiyyah* or the Greek *nothros* is slow and apathetic. Paul (Gr. *nothros*) warned the Jewish Christians "not **to become lazy.** (Heb. 6:12.) **Forced labor** renders a word (*mas* or *mis*) that means a group of people, here lazy people, who are forced to work for a government or a wealthy person or business.

The hand of the **diligent** is a hard-working, industrious person. A diligent person is characterized by care and perseverance in carrying out what needs to be done. This person is persistently industrious in carrying out his tasks. One who cares about his work as though it literally is reflective of him as a person will eventually be in a position of authority with much power, be it by his hand or by the hand of another who sees the wisdom of elevating him.

One who is lazy will find himself and his family in poverty, not having the bare necessities of life. However, with hard work, one can become rich in the bare necessities of life, which are food, clothing, shelter, and health. **Diligence** leads to wealth just as laziness leads to poverty. One of the main themes in Proverbs is the contrast between the hard worker and the lazy person. (10:4; 12:24; 13:4; 14:23; 15:19; 16:26; 18:9; 20:13; 21:17, 25-26; 28:19) Diligence as the guaranteed way (barring any unforeseen or unexpected occurrences) to gain prosperity and laziness as the quickest way to poverty. The lazy person is the foremost fool who ends up destitute. If the Jewish person became so poor, he could not survive he could sell himself into servitude until he regained enough finances to leave serving another. A lazy person, in time, will have exhausted any means of financially supporting himself, and will be in forced labor of his own volition.

PROVERBS 11:30 The Righteous One Is Capturing Souls and Is Rewarded

Proverbs 11:30 Updated American Standard Version (UASV)

³⁰ The fruit of the righteous is a tree of life,
and whoever captures souls is wise.

Proverbs 11:30 Updated American Standard Version (UASV)

³⁰ The fruit of the righteous is a tree of life, and whoever captures souls is wise.

The fruit of the righteous is a tree of life: The **righteous** person, by speech, conduct, and example, that is, **fruit** or fruitage (Heb. peri), he **captures** or wins souls, namely, by the person (soul) listening to the righteous one, he gets spiritual food, and he is then led to serve God, and he may receive the life that God makes possible. The **righteous** (Heb. *tsaddiq*) refers to one who is in a righteous standing before God, who is characterized by righteous actions and morals in accordance with God's moral standards.

and whoever captures souls is wise: The **whoever** here could very easily be the **righteous** one from line one, who **captures** (Heb. *laqach*) or wins **souls** (Heb. *nephesh*) because of his wisdom that he acquired and now obeys in his speech, conduct, and example. His speech and conduct, the righteous person, brings spiritual food to those who listen to him. They are encouraged to serve God and may ultimately receive the life that God has made possible.

Proverbs 11:31 Updated American Standard Version (UASV)

³¹ **If the righteous on earth will be rewarded,**[37] **how much more the wicked and the sinner!**

If the righteous on earth will be rewarded: The **righteous** (Heb. *tsaddiq*) refers to one who is in a righteous standing before God, who is characterized by righteous actions and morals in accordance with God's moral standards. The Hebrew word (*shillum*) rendered reward means to be given **recompense** for one's behavior or actions, that is, dispense a just penalty or reward for doing good or for doing bad; to **be repaid**, receive payment whether good or bad.

how much more the wicked and the sinner: The **Wicked** (Heb. *rasha*) is the unrighteous who are evil, being guilty of willfully and purposely violating the standards of God. In the Old Testament, it refers to the one who refuses to acknowledge or obey God. In the book of Proverbs explicitly, it refers to the foolish one who ignores or refuses to follow the divine teachings of God. It is a state or condition of evil that focuses on the violating of God's laws or standards. (Prov. 3:33; 18:3) The **sinner** (Heb. *chata*) is one who in any spoken word (Job 2:10; Ps 39:1), wrong action (Lev. 20:20; 2 Cor. 12:21) or failing to act when one should have (Num. 9:13; Jam. 4:17), in mind and heart (Prov. 21:4; Rom. 3:9-18; 2 Pet 2:12-15) that is contrary to God's personality, ways, will and purposes, standards, as set out in the Scriptures. **How much more** is referring to the fact that if the repentant righteous person is punished; then, the willful wicked person will rightly be punished much more.

The Proverb begins with a Hebrew particle (*hen*; Look!), which is rendered "if" here, it is used to call attention to an important truth that follows. The righteous person makes his best effort to live according to God's standards, but there are times when he errs. (Ecclesiastes

---

[37] Or *repaid*

7:20) Yes, he wants to do right, but sometimes stumbles and is heartbroken, and the principle, "whatever a man sows, this he will also reap," applies. (Gal. 6:7) Thus, for the righteous one's mistakes, he will be **rewarded** by being disciplined. What about the wicked person, who sins willfully and has no interest in an upright life? Certainly, he deserves a far greater **reward**, that is, a more severe punishment. The apostle Peter writes, "And 'If the righteous is scarcely saved, what will become of the godless man and the sinner?'" (1 Peter 4:18) Therefore, let us be the righteous person seeking to do his best to live according to God's standards as outlined in his Word. And if we stumble, repent and get up.

PROVERBS 9:11-12 You Will Reap What You Sow

Proverbs 9:11-12 Updated American Standard Version (UASV)

¹¹ For by me your days will be multiplied,
   and years will be added to your life.
¹² If you are wise, you are wise for yourself;
   and if you scoff, you alone will bear it.

For by me your days will be multiplied: Days being multiplied (Heb. *rabah*) are the outcome of keeping company with wisdom. It is your free will choice to do so, as you are individually responsible. Days are multiplied not through God stepping into your life and miraculously prolonging it but rather by your acquiring wisdom and being obedient.

And years will be added to your life: Do you want years to be added to your life (Heb. *chayyim*), and would you like to be certain that you are walking down the right path and your life is heading in the right direction to have the blessing and approval of God?

If you are wise, you are wise for yourself: Making the effort and buying out the time to gain wisdom is our personal responsibility. A **wise** (*chakam*) man with good judgment acts in a way that benefits himself, and he is rewarded by his own wise decisions that he makes, not by following the footsteps of others.

And if you scoff, you alone will bear it: The **scoffer** (Heb. *lits*) or ridiculer who thinks more of himself than is necessary and who has nothing but contempt and derision for others, he alone is to blame for his own difficulties in life. Indeed, he will reap what he sows. May you, then, be "attentive to wisdom." – Proverbs 2:2.

What can we expect from our acquiring wisdom? Verse 11 says, "by me your days will be multiplied, and years will be added to your life." Yes, by being intimately acquainted with wisdom, our days will be increased, "wisdom restores life to its possessor." (Eccles. 7:12) It is our responsibility to acquire biblical wisdom. As Solomon puts it, "If you are wise, you are wise for yourself; and if you scoff, you alone will bear it." In other words, if you choose wisdom as a companion, you will have the advantage of the very knowledge of God. However, if you choose to scoff at wisdom, you will reap what you sow.

PROVERBS 10:8-9 The Wise of Heart or the One Foolish of Lips

Proverbs 10:8-9 Updated American Standard Version (UASV)

⁸ The wise of heart will heed commandments,
   but the one foolish of lips[38] will be trampled down.[39]

⁹ He who walks in integrity walks securely,
   but he who makes his paths crooked[40] will be known.[41]

The wise of heart will heed commandments: Back in 6:32, the author spoke of being in **want of heart**. This is one who is inexperienced, lacking good sense and wisdom, lacking good judgment or discernment. Here we have just the opposite person who is **wise of heart**. The **heart** (Heb. *leb*) is used figuratively as the location of a person's thoughts (mind), decisions, emotions, and knowledge of what is right from wrong. Thus, a person who is **wise of heart** is one who is sensible, possessing and showing good sense and good judgment in his decision making, as well as his thoughts and actions, which enable him to determine what is right and what is wrong.

The heart is very prominent in the Scriptures, as it is mentioned about a thousand times in one way or another. By far, the great majority of its occurrences in the Scriptures, the word "heart" (Heart, *leb*) is used *figuratively*. Servants of God cannot be **halfhearted** or **in**

---

[38] I.e. the one speaking foolishly
[39] I.e. *will come to ruin*, or *will be destroyed*
[40] Or *perverts his ways*
[41] Or *will be found out*

want of heart, or even **double hearted**. (Ps 12:2; Prov. 10:13) As a reader of hearts, God can see any insincere or feigned behavior on our part. He is well aware of our actions and thinking, even when we are alone. He knows our heart condition, what we are trying to do with our lives. If our heart is good, and we love God's Word, he will know. (Josh. 1:8-9; Ps. 1:1-3; 119:97, 101, 105, and 165) A person who is **halfhearted** is lukewarmly worshiping God. (Ps 119:113; Rev. 3:16) This young man being tempted by adultery is **double hearted** (literally, with a heart and a heart), is trying to serve two masters (God and his flesh), or he is deceivingly saying one thing while thinking sinful thoughts to himself. (1 Ch. 12:33; Ps 12:2) Jesus clearly condemned such **double hearted** hypocrisy. – Matthew 15:7-8.

The wise one's **heeding** (Heb. *laqach*) of commandments means that he will be receptive to the commands, he will pay attention and obey the commands. He does this willingly. The Hebrew word (*mitsvah*) translated **commandments** was used in Proverbs 2:1; 3:1; and 4:4, where it was used in reference to the words and teachings of wisdom. **My words** refer to the Law (thoughts and ideas) that Solomon has embraced in an active faith and obedience, which he is teaching as well. The use of commandments here in this verse is referring simply to the good instruction, advice or counsel that one **receives**.

but the one foolish of lips will be trampled down: The expression foolish of lips is referring to the person who speaks foolishly or is a foolish talker. His senseless babbling will cause him to be trampled down. The Hebrew word for **fool** (*evil*) is referring to a simpleton, one who lacks good judgment. He lacks understanding and stubbornly so, who is both stupid in his actions and his words. The wise of heart is being contrasted with foolish of lips. Instead of being able to have the good judgment to recognize, let alone obey good instruction, advice or counsel that the foolish one **receives**, his senseless talk causes him to be **trampled down**, that is he will be brought to ruin. In other words, his foolish words that are spoken without thinking will bring him a lifetime of ruination, trouble, ending up with nothing.

He who walks in integrity walks securely: In the Bible, the expression "to walk" is figurative and illustrative and can mean to follow a certain course of action, as "Noah walked with God." (Gen. 6:9; 5:22) Those who walk with God follow the life course outlined by God's Word and will find his favor, that is, be pleasing to him. Pursuing such a life-course makes you different from most of the unbelievers. The Greek New Testament uses the same illustrative expression, contrasting two different courses of action sought by one before and after becoming a servant of God. (Eph. 2:2, 10; 4:17; 5:2) The Hebrew verb **walk** (*halak*) is expressing a life course that one will experience as a result of possessing the wisdom of God and the Hebrew noun **securely** (*betach*) is telling us that as compared to those ignoring or rejecting the wisdom of God, we will **walk ... securely**. This is not saying that we will absolutely be free from danger or injury but rather, Solomon is saying far more so than those who lack wisdom.

Hebrew terms relating to integrity have the root meaning of that which is "whole" or "complete." They often suggest moral soundness and uprightness. Those walking in **integrity** are unbending in devotion to Jehovah. For such blameless ones, he is a protective shield because they display true wisdom and conform to his righteous standards. This does not mean, though, that Jehovah will not allow you to be tested. He did so even with Job. "God is faithful," the apostle Paul noted to the Corinthians. In full he said, "No temptation has overtaken you but such as is common to man; and God is faithful, who will not allow you to be tempted beyond what you are able, but with the temptation will provide the way of escape also, so that you will be able to endure it." – 1 Corinthians 10:13.

but he who makes his paths crooked will be known:
Paths crooked: (Heb. *derākāy meaqqēsh*) means their ways are morally crooked, **perverse**, distorted, dishonest, and evasive when it is compared alongside the just, right and correct ways of the wise ones. The phrase "will be **known**" can be rendered will be **"found out."** The one who perverts his ways (makes his paths crooked) will be found out (known). It is likely referring to being found out by other people as opposed to being found out by God because God would have already foreseen any perverted ways. God could never find out anything.

If you are always talking; there is no opportunity to learn anything. You acquire wisdom by listening to the good instruction, advice or counsel that you receive through others. Because you are sensible, possessing and showing good sense and good judgment in your decision making, you will then accept and obey these commands. However, the simpleton foolish one is only aware of his own ignorance because he is too busy babbling to learn anything. Therefore, he will eventually bring himself to ruin and anyone else in association with him. Therefore, if you may it a practice of walking down crooked paths (perverted ways), you will eventually be **found out** by others, who will likely never trust you when the time comes when you seriously want and need others to believe and trust you, but they will feel they cannot.

PROVERBS 2:6-8 God Gives Wisdom to His Holy Ones

Proverbs 2:6-8 Updated American Standard Version (UASV)

⁶ For Jehovah gives wisdom;
   from his mouth come knowledge and understanding;
⁷ he stores up sound wisdom for the upright;
   he is a shield to those who walk in integrity,
⁸ guarding the paths of justice
   and watching over the way of his holy ones.

Jehovah represents himself symbolically as having a **mouth** (Heb. *pě(h)*) to convey to the reader about his communication, speech that gives you information, exhortation, counsel, or commands, which are contained in Scripture, wherein God speaks to you. (cf. Heb. 1:1-2; 2 Pet. 1:20-21) The **upright** (Heb. *yā·šār*) are God's true believers, his holy ones, who are diligently seeking and searching to know, love, and obey God and to live righteously as one can within their human imperfection. (Gen. 6:5; 8:21; Jer. 17:9; Rom. 5:12) You, the **holy one** is keeping the new covenant (Jer. 31.31; Heb. 8:8-12); thus, you know **wisdom**, which has served as a **shield** (Heb. *mā·ḡēn*) of defense from the offensive weapons of Satan, the world, and your own human imperfection, as you **walk** (Heb. *hā·lăḵ*) **in integrity** (Heb. *tōm*) a state of blamelessness being free of guilt, **guarding** (Heb. *nā·ṣăr*) you, making you safe from danger within your relationship with Jehovah (Ps 40:12) on the **paths of justice, watching** (Heb. *šā·măr*) over them. Hebrew terms relating to integrity have the root meaning of that which is "whole" or "complete." They often suggest moral soundness and uprightness. Those walking in **integrity** are unbending in devotion to Jehovah. For such blameless ones, he is a protective shield because they display true wisdom and conform to his righteous standards. This does not mean, though, that Jehovah will not allow you to be tested. He did so even with Job. "God is faithful," the apostle Paul noted to the Corinthians. In full he said, "No temptation has overtaken you but such as is common to man; and God is faithful, who will not allow you to be tempted beyond what you are able, but with the temptation will provide the way of escape also, so that you will be able to endure it." – 1 Corinthians 10:13.

Jehovah God will give wisdom to those, who are seeking and searching as though it were a hidden treasure. Imagine a gold mine in the side of a hill. If someone wanted enough money to have a meal or two, without working too hard, he could just pick up some specs of gold on the hillside. However, if he wanted a lifetime of meals, a life of financial security, he would be working in the mine daylight to dark. Sadly, when those searching for treasure crossed America to California in 1849, in search of gold, they soon discovered that the odds of striking it rich were ten thousand to one. It is quite different with Jehovah God, as he gives wisdom to all, "from his mouth come knowledge and understanding." Yes, God gives out wisdom free; he is the mine, for those that want to be wise.

We need to make this a part of our prayer life. The psalmist prayed, "Teach me your way, O Jehovah, that I may walk in your truth; unite my heart to fear your name." (Psalm 86:11) This is one prayer that we know will be answered. However, the answer will be based on the level that we act in harmony with our prayers. Are we willing to buy out the time to acquire wisdom, understanding, and discernment? A mere 30-60 minutes a day of Bible study will bring results that one might not have ever imagined. Are we willing to work 30 years to pay off a house, 40-45 years to receive a social security check (USA), but not 30-60 minutes a day, to acquire the wisdom of God that leads to eternal life?

PROVERBS 2:9 Understanding What is Ethically and Morally Right and What is Wrong

Proverbs 2:9 Updated American Standard Version (UASV)

9 Then you will understand righteousness and justice
  and equity, every good course;

This is true. After you have been studying the Bible for a while you begin to connect new information to things you already know. The truth of the Bible is so rational, reasonable, sensible, so interrelated, that the parts begin to fit together very quickly, and the entire purpose of God begins to become clear. As you maintain your studies, it becomes easier for you to make the right decisions that bring more happiness now. Also, your newfound wisdom will direct you away from useless, wrong life choices.

The first result from your search for wisdom is that of your finding the knowledge of God and the wisdom that he gives. (2:5-8) The second result in your quest for wisdom is that the very knowledge of God will enable you to discern, understand what is *ethically* (rules and principles in God's Word) and *morally* (moral compass that God gave you that you still possess a measure of in human imperfection) right and what is wrong. Your ability to judge what is right and wrong and act accordingly. This strong personal ethics of right and wrong in your dealings with others is described by righteousness and justice and equity. **Righteousness** (Heb. *şĕ·ḍĕq*) is when you adhere to the moral standard set out in God's Word. **Justice** (Heb. *miš·pāṭ*) is when you are free from partiality, selfishness, bias, as well as deception, where you make decisions that reflect God's sense of what is just. It is a case of fairness in your dealings with others. **Equity** (Heb. *mê·šā·rîm*) is a sense of fairness, being straight and upright, wherein you can make decisions that are **not** governed by discrimination or dishonesty. You do nothing that is sneaky, devious, deceitful, dishonest, morally uncertain.

PROVERBS 9:1-2 The Way of Wisdom

Proverbs 9:1-2 Updated American Standard Version (UASV)

9 Wisdom has built her house;
   she has hewn her seven pillars.
² She has slaughtered her beasts;[42] she has mixed her wine;
   she has also set her table.

Wisdom has built her house: In 8:34, Wisdom first refers to her **house**. It is wisdom herself, who has **built her house**, not having another do it for her.

She has hewn her seven pillars: The Greek Septuagint (LXX) has, "she has **set up** her seven pillars." The Hebrew text has **hewn** (*chatsab*), which refers to taking an ax or ax-like tool and striking an object, to cut off or out of another main object. **Pillars** are a tall vertical structure of stone or wood used as a support for a building,[43] or a portico, which is a porch or walkway leading to a house.

On the pillars, John H Walton writes, "Many theories have been put forward to explain the significance of the seven pillars of Wisdom's house. Perhaps the most notorious suggests that the previous chapters can be divided into seven speeches, but the text does not naturally divide into the desired units to make this theory work. Some interpret the significance of the number seven as indicating the seven planets known at the time; others take it as a reference to the seven creation days. However, the simplest and best explanation is to take the number

---

[42] Lit *slaughtered her slaughtering*
[43] Illustration by Dylan Karges

seven in its typical symbolic sense as indicating completeness. We are to picture a beautiful, large house."[44] The author of Proverbs is simply conveying the idea that Wisdom's home has much space and is well-made, and impressive, while the fool or the stupid one's home is found in Sheol, that is, gravedom. The number seven can be seen as the adequacy or abundance of this house, as being the right size, and having plenty for the banquet.

She has slaughtered her beasts; she has mixed her wine: Here **slaughtered** (*tabach*) simply means the killing or butchering of animals or **beasts** that have been raised specifically for food. Here mixed wine may refer to the practice of diluting wine with water. The Jewish people did not find undiluted wine as being tasteful. The wine on Passover was mixed with three parts water and one-part wine. Then, again, there was also the practice of mixing spices into the wine to give it a variety of flavors. Or, it could be that wisdom did both of these.

She has also set her table: Setting her table meant preparing it for food for a banquet. The table itself is not like the modern-day table but rather a mat or some animal hide placed on the floor. It could also be some wooden structure that is only a few inches off the floor.

We see that wisdom has built a strong house, which is ready to receive many people. It seems that the feast is ready, as the meat is there, as well as the wine, with the table being set. The question that begs to be asked at this point is, 'who are the guests that have been invited to this feast?' Feasting with wisdom from God brings about no hurt, no reproach, no regrets, but only improvement

---

[44] John H Walton, *Zondervan Illustrated Bible Backgrounds Commentary (Old Testament): The Minor Prophets, Job, Psalms, Proverbs, Ecclesiastes, Song of Songs*, vol. 5 (Grand Rapids, MI: Zondervan, 2009), 480.

oneself and the creation or formation of right motives in the heart. We in our humility need to take wisdom's discipline and thereby reject death, and instead choose life in honor and happiness.

PROVERBS 6:20-22 Principles, Teachings, and Rules are to Guide and Protect

Proverbs 6:20-22 Updated American Standard Version (UASV)

[20] My son, My child, keep the commandment of your father,
   and forsake not the teaching[45] of your mother.
[21] Bind them on your heart continually;
   tie them around your neck.
[22] When you walk, she[46] will lead you;
   when you lie down, she will watch over you;
   and when you awake, she will talk with you.

My son, My child, keep the commandment of your father: Here the Hebrew noun **commandment** (*miṣ·wā(h)*) is an authoritative direction or instruction, given as a prescription from the one with the authority or power to a person under the authority or control of another within an organization or a family. – 1 Sam. 13:13; 1 Ki 2:43.

And forsake not the teaching of your mother: The sense of **forsaking** (Heb. *nā·ṭăš*) is to abandon, to leave behind. The son would be very foolish to abandon such warm loving communication and instruction from the mother, which are the building blocks of a balanced attitude toward life.

Bind them on your heart continually: Bind ... heart is a figurative way of saying "Remember their words always"

---

[45] Or *law*

[46] Or *they will*; I.e. the commandment of your father and the teaching or law of your mother (3xs this verse)

(ERV), "Keep their words with you always" (GNT), or "always keep it in mind." (CEV)

Tie them around your neck: Tie ... neck is a figurative way of saying "keep in mind everything they tell you" (TLB), "Let [commandments and teachings] be as if they were tied around your neck" (ICB), or "and never forget it." (CEV) The neck in Bible times was where beautiful and precious ornaments were worn, such as the necklace, so you should display by way of your conduct the commandments of the father and the laws (teachings) of the mother prominently. The importance of the discipline and authority of the father and the mother (and more significantly the value of God's commandments and laws) is being emphasized by tying them around the neck.

When you walk, she will lead you: Here **she** is referring to the father's commandments and the mother's teaching, with **walk** suggesting that the son or child, or student, the one learning is behind the one who is guiding or leading, that is, the father's authoritative direction or instruction and the mother teachings, as well as God's commandments and laws.

When you lie down, she will watch over you: Again, **she** is referring to the father's commandments and the mother's teachings, with **lying down** suggesting that the son or child, or student, the one learning is being protected (**watched over**) at their most vulnerable times in life by the commands and instructions of the father and the teachings of the mother.

And when you awake, she will talk with you: Once more, **she** is referring to the father's commandments and the mother's teachings, with **when you awake** suggesting that the son or child, or student, the one learning is being guided at each new stage of their life by the commands and instructions of the father and the teachings of the mother. Here talk is not verbal communication between two people but refers to instruction, advice, or counsel that the young one receives from the parent, or that faithful servants receive from God.

Here with verse 20 through chapter 7, we begin a journey of counsel and insight that is penned to help the young over avoid sexual immorality. Throughout the Bible, obedience to parents is coupled with subjection to God. The parents of the ancient Israelites were obligated by the Law to teach their children. Moses encouraged fathers, "these words that I am commanding you today shall be on your heart. And you shall recite them to your children, and you shall talk about them at the time of your living in your house and at the time of your going on the road and at the time of your lying down and at the time of your rising up." (Deut. 6:6-7) The mother had an impact on her children as well. While she contributed to their guidance and direction, it was under the headship of the Father, she would enforce the family law. In fact, the entire Bible, from Genesis to Revelation, the reader will discover that the main educational influence is the family.

The Word of God should be deeply embedded within **the heart** of the child from the beginning, which will only happen if the parent(s) are consistent with their message. The significance of the correction and parental authority of the parent(s) (as well as God's Word) is stressed by the exhortation to **'tie them upon your neck,'** where beautiful and precious jewelry was worn. (Pro. 1:8, 9; 3:1-3; 6:20, 21) When the young child is **walking**, that is "to go about; to go to and fro" through life, she (the commandments and instructions of verse 20), will **lead** the child (Deut. 6:7) When the child **lays down** each evening, one his parents should close out his day in prayer with him, which will become a lifelong practice. A parent can share some of God's Word with their child after he **awakes**, before the start of their day. In this way, God's Word, the commands of the father, and the instruction of the mother will lay a foundation that will help the child to walk with God for life.

PROVERBS 10:29 How God Deals with You Today

Proverbs 10:29 Updated American Standard Version (UASV)

²⁹ The way of Jehovah is a stronghold to the blameless,
  but destruction to evildoers.

The way of Jehovah is a stronghold to the blameless: Here **the way** (Heb. *derek*) **of Jehovah** is how God deals with mankind and **not** to the course of life that we should follow. God's dealings with humans means safety and protection, a place of refuge for the blameless. The Hebrew word rendered **stronghold** (*maoz*) refers to a strongly fortified defensive military structure that offers safety and protection, a place of refuge. **Blameless:** (Heb. *tam, tamim*) means, "perfect, blameless, sincerity, entire, whole, complete, and full." Of course, Noah, Jacob, and Job were not literally perfect. When used of imperfect humans, the terms are relative, not absolute. However, if we are *fully* committed to following, a life course based on God's will and purposes, fully living by his laws, repent when we fall short, he will credit us righteousness.

but destruction to evildoers: The contrasting parallel here is between **stronghold** and **destruction** and between **blameless** and **evildoers**. The way of Jehovah is a destruction to evildoers. The way of Jehovah's dealings with humans, in this case, evildoers, is destruction. The evildoers refuse to live a way of life that aligns them with the Word of God and with God's personality, standards, ways, which is rebellion, the rejection of God's sovereignty.

PROVERBS 5:12-13 I Have Paid a High Price

Proverbs 5:12-13 Updated American Standard Version (UASV)

¹² and you say, "How I hated discipline,
   and my heart despised reproof!
¹³ I did not listen to the voice of my teachers
   or incline my ear to my instructors.

And you say, "How I hated discipline: Here **hated** (Heb. *sane*) has an emotion ranging from disliking intensely, abhor, detest, loathe, open hostility, antipathy or aversion towards a person or thing, but in other places it can have the weaker sense of being "set against," also being toward a person or thing. **Discipline** (Heb. *mû·sār*) is repeatedly mentioned throughout the book of Proverbs. In the Scriptures, discipline often carries the sense of correction, admonition, rebuke, or chastisement. It is the practice or methods of teaching and enforcing acceptable patterns of behavior: correction, admonition, or modification, whether it is self-discipline or the discipline of another. According to *The Expositor's Bible Commentary*, it "denotes the training of the moral nature, involving the correcting of waywardness toward folly." (Garland and Longman 2008, 48) Do we need this training? Whether we are disciplining ourselves, or are being disciplined by another, by grasping the counsel within the Scriptures, and then applying it in our lives, it moves us to become a better servant of God. If we are to move over from inherited death to life, we need discipline. – Prov. 1:3; 3:11; 5:12

And my heart despised reproof: Here the Hebrew term (*nā·'ăṣ*) for **despise** has the meaning of looking down on with contempt, to scorn, reject, spurn, strong dislike, which matches **hatred** from line 1. Here **reproof** (Heb. *tô·ḵă·ḥăṯ*) has the sense of an act or an expression of criticism or disapproval, even condemnation. It is speaking strong words of disapproval, which may also include punishment. – Ps 39:12; Prov. 1:23, 25, 30; 3:11; 5:12; 6:23; 10:17; 12:1; 13:18; 15:5, 10, 31, 32; 27:5; 29:1, 15; Ezek. 5:15.

I did not listen to the voice of my teachers: The Hebrew term (*shama*) means to **listen**, to hear, to pay close attention, and respond, heed, or obey on the basis of having heard. In other words, you did not obey the words of the instructions from the teacher or you did not pay attention to the words of the teacher.

Or incline my ear to my instructors: The Hebrew (*nā·ṭā(h)*) incline is when one leans their ear in the speaker's direction so that they can hear better. This is simply a more literary way of saying be attentive or pay attention. You need to carefully listen to the instructor and heed his words.

Regret is all you have left, so you start in with the "only If" or "why did I not." You ask yourself, why did I reject corrective counsel? Why did I not listen to my teachers? Why did I not take instructors words seriously? Why did I allow the strange woman to have her way with me? Why have I ruined my life? It is all too little too late, as I have failed to heed the voices of reason and logic. My life has been one of regret where had I listened to the teachers and instructors instead of stubbornly discarding their counsel, life would not have been one disaster after another. Now, late in life, my conscience has condemned me and my long hatred for the instructors and teachers is regretful. I have failed to obey my teachers, my instructors, and my father.

PROVERBS 11:15 Use Material Assets Wisely

Proverbs 11:15 Updated American Standard Version (UASV)

¹⁵ Whoever puts up security for a stranger will surely suffer harm,
 but he who hates striking hands in pledge is secure.

Whoever puts up security for a stranger will surely suffer harm: The Hebrew word (*ki·ā́raḇ*) rendered **put up a security** means to pledge something as collateral, make a guarantee, including yourself. **Stranger:** (Heb. *zār*) was applied to those who forsook what was in harmony with the Mosaic Law and so were estranged from God and not necessarily as some foreigner or non-Israelite. Here, like in Proverbs 6:1, it simply seems to be a contrast between someone you know (neighbor) with some you do not know (stranger). However, it is possible that the contrast could be a countryman Israelite (neighbor) with a non-Israelite (stranger). The point being made is that it is careless and unwise to make a security for, a pledge for, a deal for a total stranger of whom you have no intimate knowledge, so as to make an informed decision, or to make a pledge for one who has estranged himself from God. To make a deal for a total stranger of whom you have no knowledge of or a person who is estranged from God, this places you at the mercy of the person you are indebted for and the odds are you will suffer a loss. **Suffer harm** (Heb. *ye·roa*) refers to one who experiences injury or emotional pain. The one who offers a pledge, surety, guarantee for a stranger can be distressed, disturbed, miserable, a feeling of anxiety over the loss of whatever they had offered.

but he who hates striking hands in pledge is secure: Here **hates** (Heb. *sōnē*) is referring to one who has an intense dislike, who feels an aversion for striking hands in pledge, especially for or with a stranger. The Hebrew word (*toqeim*) translated **striking hands** is grasping hands or shaking hands with another in order to make a pledge. This person who hates striking hands is **secure** (Heb. *batach*), that is, a safe state from danger, he has no anxiety, stress over risking a pledge or losing a pledge.

In Solomon's day, borrowing and lending money was a common practice. The risk-taking investors found many opportunities to lend funds, of course, at high rates of interest, and on responsible **suretyship** (line of insurance). When one entered into such a **pledge**, it was guaranteed by **striking hands**. Only the foolish would allow a **stranger** to talk them into putting up **security** for him so he could borrow money, as this would bring on severe distress of the possibility of the stranger's disappearing, leaving you to suffer the harm, in that, it would now be your obligation to repay his loan. Solomon, in all likelihood, was thinking of his son Rehoboam when he penned this Proverb. Rehoboam was the heir apparent to the throne, who loved flattery, which the court parasites gave him in abundance for his generosity, making it foolish to give him his royal inheritance.

It is careless and unwise to make a security, a pledge, a deal for a total stranger based on a mere handshake. (Prov. 11:15; 17:18; 20:16; 22:26–27; 27:13) To make a deal for a total stranger based on a handshake alone places you at the mercy of the person you are indebted to and the neighbor. (6:1, 3) Proverbs are concise and to the point of offering responsible actions. Pledge something or self for a stranger (risky) and there will be much distress, pain and suffering over the risk until all had been repaid, and if it is not repaid, the pain and suffering will increase a thousand-fold. Avoid shaking hands, a gesture in ancient Israel that was like a signature on a contract today, and you will be free from financial or personal entrapment, and the anxiety and stress of worrying over such a foolish pledge.

Proverbs' comments about offering or giving monetary or personal help to others could help many us to avoid the stress of financial problems. There are some who are emotionally inclined to offer financial help without security or they even go surety for others. Frequently, they lose their money in this way and therefore suffer serious economic hardships. Hence, their life would be greatly improved from living in harmony with the above Biblical warning.

PROVERBS 6:1-3 Deliver Yourself from Foolish Pledges

Proverbs 6:1-3 Updated American Standard Version (UASV)

6 My son, if you have become surety for your neighbor,
   have given your pledge for a stranger,
² if you are snared in the words of your mouth,
   caught in the words of your mouth,
³ Do this then, my son, and deliver yourself,
   for you have come into the palm of your neighbor:
   go, humble yourself, plead with your neighbor.

My son, if you have become surety for your neighbor: This is a supposed or assumed situation. "My son, *suppose* you have ..." **Become surety** means to become a pledge or a guarantee, it is a person who takes responsibility for another's performance of an undertaking. The Hebrew word (ʽā·rǎḇ) means to **put up a security**, mortgage, make a guarantee, give a pledge. One pledges (promising to do) something as collateral, which can even include oneself, such as the case in Genesis 43:9, Judah says to Jacob, "I will be a pledge of his [Benjamin] safety," i.e., safe return.

Neighbor: (Heb. rēaʽ) This does not necessarily refer to someone who lives next door or near to another. The Hebrew noun generally refers to any countryman with a focus on local companions, friends, acquaintances, colleagues. It can be one who is of the same race, or social/geographical or someone who lives within your community. – Ex. 2:13; 22:6; 2 Sam. 16:17; Prov. 6:1.

Have given your pledge for a stranger: Pledge means a thing that is given as security for the fulfillment of a contract or the payment of a debt and is liable to forfeiture in the event of failure. The Hebrew literally means 'to strike tour palms (hand) with a stranger.' It is similar to making an agreement today by shaking hands on a deal. **Stranger:** (Heb. $zār$) was applied to those who forsook what was in harmony with the Mosaic Law and so were estranged from God and not necessarily as some foreigner or non-Israelite. Here it simply seems to be a contrast between someone you know (neighbor) with some you do not know (stranger). However, it is possible that the contrast could be a countryman Israelite (neighbor) with a non-Israelite (stranger). The point being made is that it is careless and unwise to make a security, a pledge, a deal with a total stranger based on a mere handshake. (Prov. 11:15; 17:18; 20:16; 22:26–27; 27:13) To make a deal with a total stranger based on a handshake alone places you at the mercy of the person you are indebted to and the neighbor. (vs. 1, 3)

If you are snared in the words of your mouth: A snare (Heb. $yā·qǎš$) brings an animal into captivity, harm, or death when it is caught in them; therefore, snares can represent causes of one's loss of freedom, or calamity, harm, or death. A servant of God must thoroughly examine and be cautious about what securities, pledges, deals that he chooses to make so that he does not find himself snared (trapped) in a situation, herein the repaying of the debt, from which escape may be very difficult or essentially impossible. (Prov. 6:1-3; 20:25)

Caught in the words of your mouth: This is repeated twice. **Caught** is similar to **snared** and renders a Hebrew verb ($lā·ḵǎḏ$), which means to capture, seize, take that implies by force and is also used of catching something in a snare or trap.

Do this then, my son, and deliver yourself: Here the Hebrew conjunction **then** transitions us from the "if" clauses of verses 1-2 into the commands of verse 3. **Do this** is basically saying that *this is what you are to do* if you wish to deliver (save) yourself. **Deliver yourself** means to save yourself, to remove yourself, to free yourself, to flee from danger, the snare.

For you have come into the palm of your neighbor: The Hebrew word (*kăp*) is rendered "hand" (ASV, ESV, NSSB) but it literally means "palm." *'In, into,* or *under the palm (hand) of someone'* means to be under their control, power or dominion. "you have come into the control of your neighbor."

Go, humble yourself, plead with your neighbor: The Hebrew verb (*rā·pās*) whose form and meaning seem to have the sense of tread on oneself, trample oneself down, or crush down. This means to act in a modest, unassuming way, having no arrogance and pride.

The proverb is warning the reader about being too quick to offer some kind of financial security for a stranger or neighbor that was not well known in the community, to place that kind of trust in him. It would be foolish to take such a risk with one's finances. This warning is not to take away from the Law that exhorted them to help their fellow Israelite brother who fell on hard times, by loaning him money without interest, helping him with food, or even taking him in for a time. (Leviticus 25:35-38) However, if the new neighbor is not well known, he could be a social misfit that does not wisely take care of his responsibilities. Then, in this case, you would be naive to risk your family's finances on such an unknown. There may have been a trustworthy Israelite neighbor, who was involving himself in a risky business venture. He may have needed more capital so he would look to his friends and neighbors to invest with him. This would be foolish too because the debt would be on those invested if the deal fell through. It is like cosigning for a house loan today. If the borrowers fail to make the payments, the cosigner is responsible for the loan.

PROVERBS 12:16 The Wise Person Pauses and Considers His Words

Proverbs 12:16 Updated American Standard Version (UASV)

16 A fool's anger is known in a day,[47]
 but the prudent man covers shame.

A fool's anger is known in a day: Fools (Heb. *kesîl*) hate knowledge as they lack good judgment. Their character is stupidity, rudeness, that is, one who completely lacks understanding, who is rebellious in his ways. (Prov. 1:22) The **Foolishness:** (Heb. *ivveleth*) of the foolish one, who has the trait of acting stupidly or rashly because he is devoid of wisdom or understanding, the Hebrew noun focusing on the evil behaviors which occur in this state. In his own eyes means that this fool thinks he is right, namely, his opinions, conduct, and behavior do not need to be corrected or improved. **In a day** is a phrase that means a very short period of time. Here it means at once.

but the prudent man covers shame: The **prudent** (Heb. **arum**) **man** is one who shows shrewdness, cleverness, craftiness, sensibility, wisdom, and good judgment in making his decisions. The prudent man has a capacity for understanding the ramification for what he says and does. His **covering** (Heb. *kese*) **shame** means that he ignores, disregards, or pays no attention to the **shame** (Heb. *qalon*), dishonor or humiliation. In other words, he is not easily provoked and remains calm in the face of a personal attack, such as an insult, scorn, or slander.

---

[47] I.e. *at once*

At times we may be slighted or insulted in one way or another. What shall we do? Retaliate? Respond in kind? No, for we are not to repay evil for evil. (Rom. 12:17-21) The foolish man angrily responds to an insult to his honor very quickly. However, the prudent man pauses long enough for a short prayer and to consider the results of responding inappropriately. He takes the time to ponder God's Word. Jesus' words: "If anyone slaps you on the right cheek, turn to him the other also." (Matthew 5:39) When he responds in such a way, he avoids escalating the tension and causing more contention that could end with more emotion or physical pain to himself or others. His failure to exercise self-control may also lead to the loss of his personal dignity.

When one overreacts to some personal affront and then acts rashly, he makes himself look foolish in the eyes of others. On the other hand, he wisely ignores confrontational remarks and actions by getting control over his tongue and holding back and irrational actions. He realizes that his honor is not worth what could result from a rash response. He lets time pass until the dishonor he felt has died down, as though it had never occurred. In doing this, he actually preserves his dignity and peace of mind. He has not allowed another to move him to resort to using disgraceful words.

The fact that the **prudent man** is shrewd, clever, and crafty does not mean that he is silently scheming his revenge. Rather, these qualities can apply in a good sense as well as a bad sense. Here, these qualities are used with knowledge and wisdom in the book of Proverbs

In Proverbs it is linked with knowledge and wisdom, with a prudent person who thinks a matter through instead of reacting just from emotion. (Prov. 13:16; 14:8; 22:3) In the face of some unjust criticism or petty insult that seems to bring dishonor, the shrewd person restrains his tongue. He remains in control, instead of letting the other person or the situation control him. And he certainly benefits from such prudence in that he thus avoids the fights that frequently come to the person who rashly responds when his feelings are hurt.

Why Pausing Before You Speak Does Not Really Work

In an online article titled 18 Ways to Keep Your Relationship Strong, it reads, "**Keep the playfulness alive.** We all love to play, regardless of our age. Do the following: have fun together; do something ridiculous together, and just let go. In addition, the next time that your partner says something that bothers you, try responding with a joke instead of getting defensive."[48] One loving woman responded to this by saying, "It is difficult to respond with a joke when something our partner said annoyed us."

Another online article says, "Here's an amazingly simple thing you can do in your daily life that can work serious wonders. Just take a slight pause before you speak."[49] This is a common thought by persons trying to help us improve our friendships as well as our relationships. However, I would say they **have only touched on half** of the answer. Without that other half of the answer, the pause really does not help. Before we offer the other half of the answer, let's take a pause to explain the obstacles that stand in our way.

There are four factors that contribute to our getting upset or angry at what someone says to us. **(1)** We are imperfect and live in an imperfect world, compounded by the fact that God's Word says we are **mentally bent and lean toward doing bad**. We read, "When the LORD saw

---

[48] 18 Ways to Keep Your Relationship Strong (Saturday, September 16, 2017) https://daringtolivefully.com/keep-your-relationship-strong
[49] Tool: Pause Before You Speak (Saturday, September 16, 2017) http://acleanmind.org/tools-techniques/tool-pause-before-you-speak/

that the wickedness of man on the earth was great and that the whole bent of his thinking was never anything but evil, the LORD regretted that he had ever made man on the earth." (Gen. 6:5, AT) **(2)** We have a wicked spirit creature, Satan the Devil, who is misleading the entire world of humankind. We read, "Be sober-minded; be watchful. Your adversary the devil prowls around like a roaring lion, seeking someone to devour." (1 Pet 5:8, ESV) **(3)** We live in a world that caters to the imperfect flesh. We read, "For all that is in the world—the desires of the flesh and the desires of the eyes and pride in possessions, is not from the Father but is from the world. And the world is passing away along with its desires, but whoever does the will of God abides forever." (1 John 2:16-17) **(4)** We are unable to understand our inner person, which the Bible informs us is wicked: "The heart is deceitful above all things and desperately sick; who can understand it?" The apostle Paul tells us, "just as sin came into the world through one man, and death through sin, and so death spread to all men because all sinned." There is only one major factor in all four parts that will have an effect on the other two, **you**. Jeremiah 17:9; Romans 5:12.

Yes, we create our own stress when someone says something that we feel is unloving or unkind. Because **(1)** we do not understand our true imperfection, and our imperfection is easily misled by point number **(2)**, Satan. Moreover, we are easily enticed by point number **(3-4)**, the world and its desires, as well as our heart. We read, "But each person is tempted when he is lured and enticed by his own desire. Then desire, when it has conceived gives birth to sin, and sin, when it is fully grown, brings forth death." (Jam 1:14-15, ESV) Only by an active faith in Christ, and a true understanding of our imperfection, can we hope to function in an imperfect world, defeat Satan, gain control over our imperfect flesh, allow God to read our heart and help us **not** to fall victim to our own desires of the eyes. Now, let us get to that second half of our Pause before you speak.

The Bible tells us that **(1)** we are mentally bent toward evil, **(2)** we have an inner heart that is treacherous, and we cannot fully understand it. This means that no human can go without ever saying something hurtful, unloving, or unkind to the people they love. It is impossible. If one of the mates has the mindset that they "should" be able to, there is no way for that person to grow in the relationship until he or she recognizes our imperfection as true. The above also has an impact on what we do when we paused before we respond.

If we just pause before we speak, our mind that is bent toward evil and our treacherous heart will feed us inappropriate thoughts, which will only upset us more. What can we do? We must pause **and reason with ourselves** during that pause. First, we need to identify when a comment to us is upsetting. We will feel a tenseness in our chest. We will feel our blood pressure rise. We will feel our heartbeat quicken. We will feel tense all over. Our mentally bent mind will begin to race with thoughts. If we feel these things, it is paramount that we **pause and ponder**. That is the second half of the answer, *ponder*. We are going to use a couple as our example. The husband has an irrational thought and before he can stop himself, he says something offensive to his wife. She immediately has the above physical, mental and emotional reaction.

Pause and Ponder

She will pause and say the following things to herself:

- What was his intent when he said that? Did he willfully mean to cause me harm? Or, is it his mentally bent imperfect mind and treacherous heart speaking?
- I know that he truly loves me very much. So, it is likely not intentional. He just misspoke.

- Every day, he expresses his love and concern. This comment is not what that loving man would say if he thought it through.

The most important equation in this **pause and ponder** is the word *intent*. The second most important equation is the person's *character*. Intent means that the mate willfully and intentionally, purposely meant to hurt his or her mate. If you deduce that the person had no intention of hurting you, it will ease your tension. Now, what is the mate's character? If the mate 95 percent of the time says loving, caring, thoughtful comments to you; then, this means his hurtful comment is out of character, not really him. If it is the mate's sinful nature, human weakness, his or her imperfection that brought about the hurtful comment, Jesus said we are to forgive him or her an unlimited number of times. We go to God every day with our sins and are very grateful that God is so gracious, so as to forgive us because we are repentant and sorry for our human weaknesses. Therefore, we should be quick to forgive others for their transgressions against us.

NOTE: This unlimited forgiving does not apply to emotional, mental, or physical spousal abuse. In this case, separation is best until the offender seeks and receives help. If the offender is unwilling to acknowledge, accept his or her abuse, as well as refusing any kind of mental health treatment; then, separation may very well become divorce.[50]

---

[50] https://christianpublishinghouse.co/2016/10/05/what-is-the-scriptural-basis-for-divorce-and-remarriage-among-christians/

PROVERBS 12:11 Meaningful Hard Work

Proverbs 12:11 Updated American Standard Version (UASV)

¹¹ He who works his land will have plenty of bread,
  but he who follows worthless things lacks heart.

He who works his land will have plenty of bread: Here **works** (Heb. *abad*) **his land** is referring to preparing the land for raising crops by plowing or cultivating. However, here it has a more basic sense of *work* or *labor* where one expends considerable energy and intensity in a task or function. Like in 12:9 **bread** (Heb. *lechem*) is representative of life's necessities, so **having plenty of bread** is saying that one who works hard will have plenty of life's basic necessities, he will never be penniless.

but he who follows worthless things is in want of heart: One **who follows worthless things** (*reqim*) is a reference to one who gives his time, labor and energy to things that are useless. There is no value, no advantage to these worthless pursuits. This person is **in want of heart**, as Solomon expresses it. The Hebrew (*chaser leb*) is rendered (interpreted) as "lacks sense" in other translations. (ESV, LEB, CSB, and NASB) This foolish person is lacking good sense and wisdom, lacking good judgment or discernment as to the worthless things that he pursues in his life.

Drawing upon yet another aspect of agricultural life, working the land, Solomon stresses that meaningful hard work will cause us to reap benefits. However, the one who is lacking good judgment or understanding (in want of heart) spends most of his time in pursuit of worthless, idle, speculative things, which have no value or advantage. The lessons in Proverbs 12:10-11 are clear: Be compassionate and hardworking.

PROVERBS 9:7-9 Be Wise and Accept Constructive Counsel

Proverbs 9:7-9 Updated American Standard Version (UASV)

7 He who corrects a scoffer gets himself abuse,
    and he who reproves a wicked man gets injury.[51]
8 Do not reprove a scoffer, or he will hate you;
    reprove a wise man, and he will love you.
9 Give instruction to a wise man, and he will be still wiser;
    teach[52] a righteous man, and he will increase in learning.

He who corrects a scoffer gets himself abuse: The verb translated **correct** (Heb. *yasar*) means to offer corrective counsel with the intention of improving the behavior of another. As discipline it need not come across as punishment, it is simply straight talk, withholding no punches, being very direct in teaching ones how to live their lives in the reverential fear of God so that they become wise from the life lessons before they are tempted by this wicked world and those alienated from God that would put them to the test.

The Hebrew word rendered **scoffer** (*lets*) is referring to someone who jeers, mocks, ridicules or treats someone with contempt. The person ridiculing another builds up resentment, anger, and hatred for the one trying to help make his path straight. Here the scoffer or ridiculer is one who resists being offered constructive correction and instruction. The **abuse** (Heb. *qalon*) is what one receives

---

[51] Lit *a blemish*
[52] Lit *make known to*

for his efforts at trying to give direction to a scoffer, which is utter contempt, disrespect, and dishonor.

And he who reproves a wicked man gets injury: This line is quite similar to the first line in meaning. **Reprove** (Heb. *yakach*) is similar in meaning to correct and has the same strong sense offering another straight talk, withholding no punches, being very direct in teaching ones how to live their life. The slight difference here with *yakach* **reprove** over *yasar* **correct** is that *yakach* carries a value judgment, implying that the one being reproved is guilty. When we look at the Hebrew word for wicked (*rasha*), we get the same implication of guilt, as the evil person is unrighteous, with a focus on the guilt of his being in violation of some standard.

Scoffers like to ridicule others, but if they are ridiculed themselves, they are unable to take it and will react badly, even violently. The wicked person has no appreciation for the one offering him reproof, to help him on the path of life. It can be very unwise to try and teach the beneficial truths of God's Word to someone who has utter contempt for you and the truth you are trying to share, for he will only ridicule your efforts. In your endeavor to reach the honest hearted with the good news of the kingdom, you need to be careful not to get too involved in debates and extensive argumentation with ridiculers.

Do not reprove a scoffer, or he will hate you: **Reprove** renders the same word that was used in 9:7b. **Scoffer** is as was used in 9:7a. **Scoffers** and **hate** are used in Proverbs 1:22, where the question is asked, "How long, O simple ones, will you love being simple-minded? And how long will scoffers delight in their scoffing and fools **hate knowledge**?"

Reprove a wise man, and he will love you: This line is the beginning of three lines (9:8b-9) that will contrast the first three lines of 9:7-8a. **Reprove** renders the same word from the previous line and that was used in 9:7b.

Truly **wise** (Heb. *chakam*) **ones** can talk frankly to each other with straight talk, holding nothing back and help each other to improve or to correct themselves where needed. The wise has a capacity for insight, understanding, and discernment. Here **love you** has the sense of respecting you.

Give instruction to a wise man, and he will be still wiser: Why will a wise person love or respect you for giving him reproof? Because he knows that through correction "he will be still wiser."

Teach a righteous man, and he will increase in learning: Increase in learning is one who continues to take in knowledge. No one is too wise or too old to keep learning.

If we are to be taught by wisdom, there will be times when we must accept correction and reproof. Of course, most of us tend to bristle at such times, yet it becomes easier as we mature in the faith. A scoffer is a ridiculer, one who expresses derision or scorn about somebody or something. This one does not receive correction well at all and has a dislike of anyone so offering. The wicked are in a whole other category, as they are blinded by their hatred for others, especially anyone suggesting they need help.

Therefore, it is a waste of time to attempt to offer 'what is holy [Scriptural wisdom] to dogs or throw your pearls [Scriptural wisdom] in front of pigs, lest they trample them with their feet, and turn around and tear you to pieces.' (Matt. 7:6) These ones will only ridicule any attempt that we make at sharing the good news with them. We can look to the apostle Paul, who while teaching some Jews in Antioch, came across some, who just wanted to do nothing but contradict him. What was Paul's response? He told them "since you thrust [Scripture] aside and judge yourselves unworthy of eternal life, behold, we are turning to the Gentiles." Acts 13:45-46

There will come times when we are trying to share the good news, and they will look to just debate, criticize, and argue with us. If it is they alone, it would be best just to walk away, letting it be their loss. However, if it is a public place of some sort, and others are listening intently at how you answer the challenges, it may be best to offer a reasonable answer, then express that you are not here to argue, and walk away. If you had not offered the parting answer, the others may have thought you did not have an answer.

The Christian is to be different from the world of humankind that surrounds them. As a disciple of Christ, we need to cultivate a love for discipline. The Word of God corrects us every time we pick it up. Yes, it is difficult to hear where we are falling short, but we should never be offended by correction, even if it is coming from a human representative of God. For some who have years on them, they may believe that with gray hair, they are wise from life experience. Even so, the Bible is filled with knowledge, understanding, and wisdom, from God, who has no beginning, and we will never live long enough, that we do not need counsel from time to time.

PROVERBS 11:16 The Enduring Honor of a Gracious Godly Person

Proverbs 11:16 Updated American Standard Version (UASV)

¹⁶ A gracious woman attains honor,
 and ruthless men take hold of wealth.

The discussion around this verse has been about what exactly is being contrasted here. Is the contrast between **graciousness** and **ruthlessness** so as to attain or take hold of something, between **women** and **men**, or between **honor** and **wealth**? It should be noted as well that it is only here in this verse in Proverbs that men are contrasted with women.

A gracious woman attains honor: The Hebrew word (*chen*) rendered **gracious** is an attractiveness about a person that interests or pleases others, such as being courteous, kind, and pleasant, elegant, and tasteful. The woman here is lovely, graceful, elegant, and attractive. Such a woman attains **honor** (Heb. *kabod*), that is, high praise and respect because of her good name or reputation.

and ruthless men take hold of wealth: Ruthless (Heb. *arits*) men are cruel, fierce, acting very harsh, and having no mercy or pity for another. These men instill terror or fear in others. **Riches** (Heb. *ashar*) refers to an abundance of material possessions and resources. It is having possessions, finances, and resources above and beyond the norm, with an emphasis on **wealth**.

The contrast here is between the enduring honor that a gracious godly woman may attain and the fleeting, temporary, momentary riches (wealth) that a ruthless man takes hold of (acquires). The book Proverbs and the Psalms show us that wisdom, common sense, good judgment and the choice of the right words give a person value and charm. (Proverbs 3:21-22; 4:7-9; 22:11; Psalm 45:1-2) This is true of a man or a woman. And the truly genuine woman of God who attains true honor through her wisdom, her reasonableness, sensibleness, shrewdness and the wise use of her tongue will receive **honor**. She will achieve honor in the eyes of God, her husband, and her family, and she will be well spoken of by others. Proverbs 22:1 says: "A good name is to be chosen rather than great riches ..." The good name of a truly genuine worshiper has enduring, eternal value in the eyes of our God.

Then, the Proverb contrasts that with the ruthless man, and elsewhere God's Word categories such ones as wicked men and men who are adversaries of God's true servants. (Job 6:23; 27:13) Ruthless men seek to harm God's people and "do not set God before themselves." (Psalm 54:3) In this imperfect fallen world, such men by overpowering and taking advantage of the innocent, they may "pile up silver like dust itself." (Job 27:16, 19; compare Luke 12:16-21) The ruthless man has taken hold of riches and has placed his trust in wealth, this confidence is seriously misplaced, for it is momentary at best. Later in the same chapter of Proverbs, we read: "He who trusts in his riches will fall." – Proverbs 11:28.

Hence, Proverbs 11:16 should wake us up to a very important lesson. The ruthless man's riches, which may at this moment seem like a mark of success in Satan's world, yet there is no value in the eyes of God. However, it is possible to find favor with God. The honor attained by those fearing God is exemplified by the history of women servants, such as Sarah, Ruth, Abigail, Esther, and Mary.

PROVERBS 19:21 Human Plans Failing as God's Purpose Succeeds

Proverbs 19:21 Updated American Standard Version (UASV)

[21] Many are the plans in the heart of a man,
   but it is the purpose of Jehovah that will stand.

Many are the plans in the heart of a man: Here the Hebrew word (*machashebeth*) rendered **plans** is a series of steps that he intends to carry out or goals that he desires to accomplish. It can be a scheme as rational or irrational thought. In Biblical Hebrew, the Hebrew word for **heart** (*leb*) has twenty-four different meanings. As in many cases, in Hebrew, the heart here is referring to the mind. The sense is the place of the person's thoughts (mind), volition (will, wish, want, desire), emotions, and knowledge of right from wrong (conscience), translated by some as **mind**.

but it is the purpose of Jehovah that will stand: The Hebrew word (*etsah*) rendered **purpose** here is similar in meaning to plans from line 1. It is a series of steps that he intends to carry out or goals that he desires to accomplish. The Hebrew word (*qum*) render **stand** means that it will be in effect and remain in force. Regardless of the plans or schemes by humans that meet with success or failure, the will and purpose of God will take place.

The wise observation as made about 3,000 years ago and as recorded in the Hebrew Old Testament of the Holy Bible remains uncontestable even today. It is found here in Proverbs 19:21:

Human plans, schemes, and devices have increased more and more rapidly through the past centuries and millenniums, but have they succeeded in standing firm, being beneficial to humanity, and producing permanent gains and controls? Where today are the greatest empires of humanity of long ago? What happened to ancient Egypt, Assyria, Babylonia, Medo-Persian, Grecian, Rome, and the British Empire that once controlled one-fourth of the earth's surface and a fourth of its population? Their glory is no more.

On the other hand, the will and purposes of God are moving along just as he has planned. They have stood firm, are unchanged, and will continue to move forward until they have success. The kingdom of God is still being proclaimed and the end of wickedness and suffering is on the horizon. Humans make plans every day but there is no guaranteed success. However, success is far more likely if our plans are in harmony with the will and purposes of God.

PROVERBS 8:35-36 Finding Life

Proverbs 8:35-36 Updated American Standard Version (UASV)

³⁵ For whoever finds me finds life
and obtains favor from Jehovah,
³⁶ But he who misses me injures his own soul;
all those who hate me love death."

For whoever finds me finds life: Do you want to find a long life? Then you need to find wisdom. **Finding** (Heb. *motsa*) here is not used in the sense of discovering something that is lost but rather in that you are finding a long life or acquiring a long life. (Prov. 3:2)

And obtains favor from Jehovah: Here obtaining **favor** (Heb. *ratson*) means that one is found favorable, acceptable in the eyes of Jehovah

But he who misses me injures his own soul: The Hebrew term rendered **misses** (*chata*) means to sin, missing the mark or the way, to go astray. It can be rendered, "he who **sins** against me." Injure (Heb. *chamas*) here means that the person is bringing about physical or moral violence against himself.

All those who hate me love death: Here **hated** (Heb. *sane*) has an emotion ranging from disliking intensely, abhor, detest, loathe, open hostility, antipathy or aversion towards a person or thing, but in other places it can have the weaker sense of being "set against," also being toward a person or thing. **Love death** is offering more detail on **injure** in line one, as those who sin against wisdom unrepentantly will end up facing eternal death.

Does it not show disrespect of wisdom's counsel, when servants of God acknowledging that they are his servants, yet they seek a means of begging off from listening to the voice of wisdom? It is likely that Christ is really personified as Wisdom from verses 22-26, and he is the one that offered himself as a ransom for us, so that we may have life. We need to listen to the voice of wisdom!

We certainly have many things in this age to captivate our attention, and we could seek out entertainment endlessly. However, if we allow the bells and whistles [non-essential features] of this wicked fallen world to distract us from pursuing God with our whole heart, mind, soul, and strength, we will eventually stumble out of the faith. How does God's Word help us in this matter? What is the balance that we need to look for and apply? First, we need to remember that eternal life is our future; where there will be an eternity to consider entertainment, i.e., pleasure. We need to understand that for now, pleasure is but momentary. Some people have a job that they love, so it is as though they never have to work, because it is such a joy, and it is a career. However, we have been given a far greater work, in that we are to preach the gospel. Jesus said, "this gospel of the kingdom will be proclaimed in the whole inhabited earth for a testimony to all the nations, and then the end will come." (Matt. 24:14) How is the end to come, if the work we have been assigned is shelved, because we are more focused on ourselves? Jesus commanded that we "go and make disciples of all the nations ... teaching them to observe everything I have commanded you." – Matthew 28:19-20.

Here is how we should use entertainment in this fallen world, or until the return of Christ. We as humans were created to enjoy pleasurable things, and having a good time is truly required, as we need to be happy, and find joy in life. However, we need to use it as a means of refreshing ourselves for the work we have been commanded to accomplish. Thus, our ministry should be our primary work, which is a heavy responsibility that can wear us down at times. Therefore, we need to be recuperated, so that we can continue our work. Thus, we use entertainment, as a means to refresh ourselves for the true work.

We are being used by God, to find those, whose hearts are disposed toward life, and help them to discover the path of salvation. As Paul said to Timothy, we are to 'fix your attention on ourselves and on our teaching. Continuing in them, for by doing this we will save both ourselves and those who hear us.' (1 Tim. 4:16) 'For we are God's fellow workers; we are God's field, God's building.' (1 Cor. 3:9) Listen to Paul, "I have shown you with respect to all things that by working hard in this way it is necessary to help those who are in need, and to remember the words of the Lord Jesus that he himself said, 'It is more blessed to give than to receive.'" (Acts 20:35) Our work in the ministry gives our lives true meaning, and it 'makes God's heart glad, and gives him an answer for those who reproach him.' Satan has slandered God, raised issues that are being settled, and he has besmirched his great name. (Prov. 27:11) If we are devoted workers to the work we have been assigned, using entertainment, to refresh us for that work, when Jesus returns we are truly going to know what happiness is, for "godliness is profitable for everything, because it holds promise for the present life and for the life to come." – 1 Timothy 4:8.

PROVERBS 12:25 Kind Words Are Healthy to Self and Others

Proverbs 12:25 Updated American Standard Version (UASV)

²⁵ Anxiety in a man's heart weighs him down,
  but a good word makes him glad.

Anxiety in a man's heart weighs him down: The Hebrew term (*deagah*) rendered anxiety means an emotion or feeling or restlessness or worry, an emotion of distress, in high anticipation of something in the future. Here the **heart** (Heb. leb) of the anxious man is a reference to the thinking, the mindset, or nature of one who worries endlessly and needlessly, always anxious over something. This is so much the case that it **weighs** him **down**, that is, literally "bows him down," in the sense that he is always sad, even depressed, feeling that life has turned against him.

but a good word makes him glad: The Hebrew word (*tob*) translated **good** in this context has the sense of good **words** from family, friends, or a coworker, or a healthcare worker that are *reassuring*, *encouraging*, or *helpful*. **Makes him glad** means that these good words raise his spirits, his mental disposition so that he is *happy* or finds *joy*, i.e., *cheers him up*.

Anxiety in your heart can be damaging to one's well-being. It can lead to depression, robbing you of strength and the initiative to take care of things that lead to a joyful and happy life. Many are the anxieties of this imperfect life in this fallen world and concerns that can **contribute** (nothing causes anxiety) to the heart being weighed down with sadness. What we need to have the burden lightened and make the heart rejoice is a **good word** of support, reassurance, and encouragement from an empathetic person. However, how can others know the intensity of the anxious distress in our heart unless we open up to them and talk about it? Yes, when we experience distress or depression, we need to confide in an understanding person who can help. Moreover, when we put our feelings into words, it relieves some of our heart's anguish. Therefore, it is good to trust in a marriage mate, a friend, or a compassionate and spiritually qualified friend from the Christian congregation.

PROVERBS 13:15 Hate What God Hates

Proverbs 6:16-19 Updated American Standard Version (UASV)

[16] There are six things that Jehovah hates,
   seven that are an abomination of his soul:
[17] haughty eyes, a lying tongue,
   and hands that shed innocent blood,
[18] a heart that devises wicked plans,
   feet that quickly to run to evil,
[19] a false witness who breathes out lies,
   and one who sows discord among brothers.

The arrangement of six things … seven is a Hebrew literary device, which tells us that this is not the entirety of what Jehovah hates or sees as an abomination, just the top seven. The first five of these qualities are body parts, which star with the head and move down to the feet (eyes, tongue, hands, heart, feet). Our final two qualities are a false witness and one who causes trouble for other.

The **haughty eyes** belong to one who is proud, conceited, possessing qualities such as stubbornness and arrogance. This is a person that sees himself as the pinnacle of everyone, who would not even consider lowering his arrogant gaze before Jehovah himself. The **lying tongue** belongs to one who continuously deceives others with his misleading utterly false information, which causes others to arrive at a mistaken belief. This is a person that could care less about the destruction of his lies in the wake of his deception. The distortion of the truth is this one's means of making the world mold to his perception of things. He could never accept the moral values of right and wrong set out in Scripture because he has distorted the truth so much that his moral compass is unable to point toward truth.

The **hands that shed innocent blood** belong to a person that has anger issues that could lead to the loss of life one day if the opportunity presented itself. He has no regard for the gift of human life that the Creator so gracious gave humankind. This person is easily enraged over any perceived insult to his person and will not hesitate to do bodily harm.

The **heart [mind] that devises wicked plans** belongs to a person that looks out for no one but himself. His motive of operation is to come out on top in life, regardless of how many people he must step on to get there. He will live within the rules of society when things are going his way but will not hesitate to go outside of those rules when it is convenient, which makes him extremely dangerous.

The **feet that hurry to run to evil** belong to a person that looks toward sin with pleasure, having ceased to feel moral pain. He literally sins with greediness, always looking for more ways to feed his pleasure centers. You have the burglar that breaks into the house to steal valuables, and then you have the vandal-burglar that breaks into the house to do damage for the thrill of it and steals something because it came to his attention in the process.

The **false witness who breathes lies** belong to a person that lies as easily as he takes a breath and has no pause in bearing false witness under oath, or in life. The one who **sends out discord between brothers** belong to a person that takes pleasure in causing trouble with his family and friends. Both of these last two persons cause havoc on society from the friend, to the family, to the community, as well as the court of law.

PROVERBS 12:9 Living Within Our Means

Proverbs 12:9 Updated American Standard Version (UASV)

9 Better to be lowly and have a servant
 than to play the great man and lack bread.

Better to be lowly and have a servant: This is literally "Better despised and a servant to him." When translated, we have "Better to be despised and have a servant." The Hebrew word (qalah) that is rendered **lowly** means to be **lightly esteemed**, to be despised, to be a nobody, to be degraded, that is, referring to a person who is considered to be of very low status in life. When we are thinking of one having little means being of a low station in life and at the same time have a servant, we should not impose our Western modern-day thinking on the historical setting of 2,800 years ago. Even today, a working-class person in South America can afford to have a maid because of the extreme poverty of others within their country. For example, in Chile, there are no social services that will care for the poor so the extremely poor will have to look for work in serving others who or of the working class. In Bible times, a nation may be conquered and devastated so those people will sell themselves into servitude of other persons of modest mean only seeking food and shelter.

than to play the great man and lack bread: Here **to play the great man** literally means "one who makes himself heavy," which refers to one who honors himself. This is a person who thinks more of himself than he ought to, which moves him to spend all of his financial resources on this false façade, trying to live a high social status. He does this to the point where he cannot even afford **bread**, the bare necessities of life. He is literally destitute. **Lacks bread**

is a way of saying one is living in poverty, lacking the basics of life's necessities, penniless.

Yes, a man of good sense is praised. However, here we are being taught that we should value humility and that simplicity is better than having a false display of feelings, attitudes, or intentions. It seems that Solomon is telling us that it is better to be a humble person of little means, having merely one servant, as opposed to spending all that you have, which would care for your life's necessities (lacking bread), in your effort to try and maintain some false pretense, trying to maintain a high social status. This is sound advice for us, as we need to live within our means. It is better to be a person who lives a moderately comfortable life, having one servant, than to be one who lives beyond his means, really having nothing.

PROVERBS 11:10-13 The Upright Bring Peace and Well-being While Wicked Sow Disorder, Corruption, and Moral Decline

The Great Joy of Your Neighbor

Proverbs 11:10 Updated American Standard Version (UASV)

¹⁰ When it goes well with the righteous, the city rejoices, and when the wicked perish there is joyful shouting.

When it goes well with the righteous, the city rejoices: When ... well is referring to God's people, the righteous, and their happiness as they prosper in life, having an abundance, wealth. The sense is their succeeding or having success. The **righteous** (Heb. *tsaddiq*) person is a just person, innocent, in the right, upright and devout in all that his thoughts, words, and actions. He lives according to the moral standard of God's Word, which is why has successes and succeeds. The **city** (Heb. *qiryah*) here is not a reference to the city itself as a whole but rather to the individuals within that city. Rejoice (Heb. *alats*) is to exult, to feel extreme happiness or elation, in a state of joy.

and when the wicked perish there is joyful shouting: Perish (Heb. *abad*) means that the wicked man is dead, destroyed, annihilated, or ruined, lost, having no kind of impact on anyone or the city. The Hebrew word rendered **wicked** (*rasha*) man here is an unrighteous man that is evil, with the focus on his guilt of violating God's standards. **Joyful shouting** (Heb. *rinnah*) is a cry of jubilation, a cry of great joy

How are we to understand Proverbs 11:10? Well, the **righteous person**, who is just, innocent, living a life that is right, and who is upright and devout in all that his thoughts, words, and actions. He lives according to the moral standard of God's Word, which is why he makes his neighbors and others within the city happy. On the other hand, there is no one within the city, who is happy with or fond of the wicked person. An evil, cruel person, who violates God's standards brings ostracism upon himself. (Proverbs 11:17) Moreover, when the wicked person dies, there is no one in the city who is mourning him. At the second coming of Christ, there will be no sorrow when he and his myriad of angels destroy the wicked. Rather, there will be great joy at their being removed from the lives of the righteous, so they can live in peace. How are we living a life that contributes to the joy of others? We do well to reflect on whether our words and actions contribute to the joy of others.

The Upright Bring Peace and Well-being While Wicked Sow Disorder, Corruption, and Moral Decline

Proverbs 11:11 Updated American Standard Version (UASV)

¹¹ By the blessing of the upright a city is exalted,
  but by the mouth of the wicked it is overthrown

By the blessing of the upright a city is exalted: Blessing: (Heb. *berakah*) When it refers to God blessing a human it is pronouncing good or showing favor, having favorable circumstances or state at a future time (Gen. 1:22), for those who have a righteous standing before him. The **upright** (Heb. *yāšār*) are God's true believers, his holy ones, who are diligently seeking and searching to know, love, and obey God and to live righteously as one can within their human imperfection. In this context **exalted** (Heb. *rum*) means that the lives of people of the city have benefited or improved to better (higher) conditions because of the blessings the upright has brought upon them.

but by the mouth of the wicked it is overthrown: Here the **mouth** (Heb. *peh*) of the wicked can be a reference to worthless, obscene, and hurtful talk, gossip, and idle chatter, or slander. The Hebrew word rendered **wicked** (*rasha*) here is an unrighteous man that is evil, with the focus on his guilt of violating God's standards. **Overthrown** (Heb. haras) here is in referred to the people of the city again, in that, they have been destroyed or ruined by the presence of the mouth of the wicked. In other words, the mouth of the wicked has offset any blessings the upright might have bestowed on citizens because of their presence.

The upright citizens within a city bring peace and well-being by building others up either through prayers or as a side effect of their presence and God blessing these upright ones. Thus, the city is exalted in that it prospers both financially and the happiness, comfort, and security of its members. On the other hand, the mouth of the wicked who bring about worthless, obscene, and hurtful talk, gossip, and idle chatter, or slander cause unrest, unhappiness, disunity, and trouble. This is even more so the case if they hold a prominent position within the city. This causes disorder, corruption, and moral decline and even economic deterioration.

Common Sense and Our Speech

Proverbs 11:12 Updated American Standard Version (UASV)

¹² He who belittles his neighbor is in want of heart, but a man of understanding remains silent.

He who belittles his neighbor is in want of heart: The Hebrew word (*buz*) rendered belittles refers to one who despises others, looks down on them with contempt, who may even verbally assault others. This person is **in want of heart,** as Solomon expresses it. The Hebrew (*chaser leb*) is rendered (interpreted) as "lacks sense" in other translations. (ESV, LEB, CSB, and NASB) This arrogant person is lacking good sense and wisdom, lacking good judgment or discernment in his life.

but a man of understanding remains silent: Proverbs many times warns about the foolishness of saying too much and the wisdom of watching your words or remaining **silent** (Heb. *charash*), as many words will eventually lead to the moment when they become hurtful words.

The harm that comes from many words is inevitable. This is especially true of one who is in want of heart or lacking good judgment (common sense). No one should say hurtful things or reveal confidential matters through unguarded speech. If we were to do so, we would lose people's trust. There may be times when we feel the urge to belittle, disparage, demean, or deride our neighbor, a friend, family members, church members, or coworkers, as maybe we have some contempt for another. Maybe we feel that the person is beneath consideration, worthless, or deserving scorn. However, such a verbal assault would only divulge our lack of good judgment or common sense, literally in want of heart or lacks heart. This person's mindset is missing something deep down within his soul, as he feels superior to those he condemns with his rhetoric.

Such a person in "want of heart" is one who does not care about consequences of what he says. In some cases, it is the person showing a bad motive, but he also reveals a want of appreciation. He attempts to ignore the penalties or consequences, which will not save him from them. On the other hand, a man of understanding has the wisdom and insight to see the end result of unguarded words and so he restrains himself in such a time.

Being Loyal to Fellow Servants of God

Proverbs 11:13 Updated American Standard Version (UASV)

¹³ He who goes about as a worker of slander reveals secrets,
but he who is trustworthy in spirit covers over a matter.

He who goes about as a worker of slander reveals secrets: One who is a **worker of slander** (talebearer) attacks the reputation of another through bad reports. Gossip is idle personal talk, which is groundless rumor and more or less harmless. **Slander** (Heb. *rakil*), on the other hand, is defamation that is made public, which is generally malicious. Slander is always damaging and destructive and always causes offense, hurt and contention. **Reveals secrets** is what a slanderer does, spreading harmful information about another person, spoken in an open, public setting, which is different than a gossiper, who spreads harmful information about another person, as a semi-private, hushed communication.

but he who is trustworthy in spirit covers over a matter: The contrast here from line one is trustworthiness. He who is **trustworthy** in spirit (Heb. *ne·eman*) has a strong allegiance to another. He is faithful and loyal, reliable, which makes him dependable. This person **covers over** or keeps information private about another for the sake of others. He is able to keep secrets confidential.

In looking at Proverbs 11:12-13 together, we can see what harm comes from one who is in want of heart (lacking common sense or good judgment) He has no concern over his lose talk to the point of where it becomes slander or abusive speech. On the other hand, a man who has understanding knows when to remain silent. Instead of revealing secrets he overs over the matter. This man of understanding is trustworthy, for he knows that an unguarded tongue can cause much harm, so he is trustworthy in spirit, being trustworthy in spirit. He is loyal to his fellow servants of God and so he does not reveal secret matters that have been shared with him in confidence. The integrity of this person is a blessing to God's people.

Bibliography

Anders, Max. 2005. *Holman Old Testament Commentary - Proverbs* . Nashville: B&H Publishing.

Archer, Gleason L. 1982. *New International Encyclopedia of Bible Difficulties, Zondervan's Understand the Bible Reference Series.* Zondervan Publishing House: Grand Rapids, MI.

Brand, Chad, Charles Draper, and England Archie. 2003. *Holman Illustrated Bible Dictionary: Revised, Updated and Expanded.* Nashville, TN: Holman.

Bromiley, Geoffrey W., and Gerhard Friedrich. 1964-. *Theological Dictionary of the New Testament, ed. Gerhard Kittel, vol. 4.* Grand Rapids, MI: Eerdmans.

Elwell, Walter A, and Philip Wesley Comfort. 2001. *Tyndale Bible Dictionary.* Wheaton: Tyndale House Publishers.

Elwell, Walter A. 2001. *Evangelical Dictionary of Theology (Second Edition).* Grand Rapids: Baker Academic.

Elwell, Walter A., and Barry J. Beitzel. 1988. *Baker Encyclopedia of the Bible.* Grand Rapids, MI: Baker Book House.

Garland, David E., and Tremper III Longman. 2008. *The Expositor's Bible Commentary: Proverbs-Isaiah.* Grand Rapids, MI: Zondervan.

Garrett, Duane A. 1993. *Proverbs, Ecclesiastes, Song of Songs, The New American Commentary, vol. 14.* Nashville: Broadman & Holman Publishers.

Goldberg, Louis. 2000. *Practical Wisdom of Proverbs.* Grand Rapids: Kregel Publications.

Mounce, William D. 2006. *Mounce's Complete Expository Dictionary of Old & New Testament Words.* Grand Rapids, MI: Zondervan.

Reyburn, William David, and Euan McG. Fry. 2000. *A Handbook on Proverbs, UBS Handbook Series.* New York: United Bible Societies.

Swanson, James. 1997. *Dictionary of Biblical Languages with Semantic Domains: Hebrew (Old Testament).* Oak Harbor: Logos Research Systems.

Terry, Milton S. 1883. *Biblical Hermeneutics: A Treatise on the Interpretation of the Old and New Testaments.* Grand Rapids: Zondervan.

Vunderink, R. W., and Geoffrey W. Bromiley. 1979–1988. *The International Standard Bible Encyclopedia, Revised (, .* Grand Rapids, MI: Wm. B. Eerdmans.

Walton, John H. 2009. *Zondervan Illustrated Bible Backgrounds Commentary (Old Testament): The Minor Prophets, Job, Psalms, Proverbs, Ecclesiastes, Song of Songs, vol. 5.* Grand Rapids, MI: Zondervan.

Wilson, Lindsay. 2018. *Proverbs: An Introduction and Commentary (Tyndale Old Testament Commentaries).* Downers Grove, IL: InterVarsity Press.

Wood, D R W. 1996. *New Bible Dictionary (Third Edition).* Downers Grove: InterVarsity Press.

www.ingramcontent.com/pod-product-compliance
Lightning Source LLC
Chambersburg PA
CBHW060157050426
42446CB00013B/2869